STILL COMPLAINING

STILL COMPLAINING

BY JIM FOSTER

A HOUNSLOW BOOK
A MEMBER OF THE DUNDURN GROUP
TORONTO › OXFORD

Publisher: Anthony Hawke
Copy-editor: Natalie Barrington
Design: Bruna Brunelli
Printer: University of Toronto Press

Canadian Cataloguing in Publication Data

Foster, Jim (James E.)
    Still complaining

ISBN 0-88882-241-3

1. Canadian wit and humor (English). I. Title.

PS8561.O77427S75 2001   C818'.5402   C2001-902371-5
PR9199.3.F573S75 2001

1   2   3   4   5   05   04   03   02   01

THE CANADA COUNCIL | LE CONSEIL DES ARTS
FOR THE ARTS | DU CANADA
SINCE 1957 | DEPUIS 1957

Canada

ONTARIO ARTS COUNCIL
CONSEIL DES ARTS DE L'ONTARIO

We acknowledge the support of the **Canada Council for the Arts** and the **Ontario Arts Council** for our publishing program. We also acknowledge the financial support of the **Government of Canada** through the **Book Publishing Industry Development Program, The Association for the Export of Canadian Books**, and the **Government of Ontario** through the **Ontario Book Publishers Tax Credit** program.

Printed and bound in Canada.⊕
Printed on recycled paper.
www.dundurn.com

Dundurn Press	Dundurn Press	Dundurn Press
8 Market Street	73 Lime Walk	2250 Military Road
Suite 200	Headington, Oxford,	Tonawanda NY
Toronto, Ontario, Canada	England	U.S.A. 14150
M5E 1M6	OX3 7AD	

TABLE OF CONTENTS

PROLOGUE

For my first book I wrote an "Introduction," but it didn't win me a Giller. I'll see how I make out with a prologue.

Yes, I'm still complaining. Well of course I am, it's my job. It's been over a year since my first book of columns came out and not a damned thing has changed. The oil companies are still ripping us off at the pumps. The Feds are still charging the GST. The Ontario Sales Tax is still there. Did the politicians not pay any attention to me at all?

I tried so hard to convince Ottawa and Queen's Park to follow my guidance. My first book, *I Hate to Complain, But* ..., was just chock-full of expert advice, but they have done nothing. I can't understand it. Surely the Prime Minister must have read it. He sure as hell wasn't doing much else — unless you call golfing with Tiger Woods or running off at the mouth in Jerusalem, "doing something."

As for Harris, he's a lost cause. He didn't even buy my book. Well he wouldn't have read it anyway; it didn't have any bunny rabbits in it. If Mike had read half of what I said about him, the OPP would be surrounding my house and I'd be banned from every golf course in Ontario. (Actually I have but it has nothing to do with Mike. I'm a spray hitter.)

I've had an off-again on-again love affair with the provincial Conservatives ever since the Grinch from the North took over. One moment I would actually start to think he was doing a passable job, then he would go and spoil it by pulling some bonehead stunt like attacking welfare mothers or closing down a hospital.

Mike was always good for a column and then what does he do? He resigns. I think I read the other day that his pension is only worth

$900,000. How's the poor guy going to live on that pittance? Maybe he should become a writer. That's where the big money is.

My first book was an overwhelming success, particularly here in Orillia. Why, people from all over the city drop by every day to borrow a copy. One guy actually intends to scout the local garage sales next summer to see if he can find a used one for 50 cents.

So much has happened to me since *I Hate to Complain, But ...* hit the bookstores. I have been besieged with offers from a number of the big American publishers to sign lucrative contracts. Currently, my agent is negotiating with The Book of the Month Club, a well-known U.S. company. They are still discussing terms, but at the moment the arrangement is, I buy six books for $1.99 U.S. and the Club will throw in a free tote bag.

Publishers Clearing House notified me this morning that the lucky number they assigned to me has miraculously appeared on the final awards list for a cash prize of close to $10,000,000. Although the win is not actually guaranteed, I am confident I will survive the final cut and have so far written post-dated cheques totalling several hundreds of thousands of dollars. As of the latest communiqué, the list of potential winners has been narrowed down to me and every American over the age of 18.

I have to go, I just heard the mailman. Maybe it's my 10 million.

With all the money he makes as Frasier, why would Kelsey Grammer want to play Shakespeare? Of course, I've always wanted to play Richard Gere's role in Pretty Woman *and chase Julia Roberts all over the Regent Beverly Wilshire Hotel.*

MacFrasier — Shakespeare for the couch potato

I read an interesting article last week that said Kelsey Grammer (he's Frasier Crane to you couch potato persons who never read the credits) will be playing Macbeth at a Shakespearean festival this summer.

Macbeth is a great role for someone like William Hutt or Sir Laurence Olivier, but it could be a disaster for a TV star. Playing any of the classics on stage is quite a challenge for TV actors and actresses. Once we have watched them in a long-running sitcom or dramatic series, it is hard for us to identify with them in some other role. We keep expecting them to do something from their show. Can't you picture Jackie Gleason as Ralph Kramden playing Marc Anthony?

"One of these days, Brutus, 'POW' right in the kisser."

What if someone cast Roseanne Barr as the fair Juliet?

"Romeo, Romeo, Wherefore art thou, Romeo?"
"I'm down here. Now get off and call 911."

I'm sure Kelsey Grammer will have a fine time running around the castle stabbing people and saying "forsooth" and "gazooks", but the audience won't really believe him. They will laugh uproariously in all the wrong places. Every time he opens a door, his TV fans will chuckle away expecting him to catch Daphne in her underwear or Bulldog and Roz swimming in the moat.

Kelsey's a TV comedian. He's not supposed to be in Scotland scheming and plotting murder with Mrs. Macbeth. He's supposed to be sipping café lattes in an upscale coffee shop with his brother, Niles, discussing why Maris wore a deep-sea diver's suit to bed on their wedding night and whether that suggests early signs of frigidity. We would be so confused we could never be able to follow the plot.

Watching Shakespeare is hard enough for us peasants without trying to understand 14th century gag lines and waiting for someone to throw a custard pie that never comes.

None of us who studied Shakespeare in high school really knew for sure what the man was talking about. We had to take the word of an English teacher. I suspect most of them didn't have a clue either and were just taking a wild guess. Even the names of his characters were weird. For instance, how many people do you know with names like Rosencrantz and Guildenstern? I think old Bill was trying to make a few extra bucks by advertising a German beer. "Try Rosencrantz Lite!"

On the other hand, now might be time to hire a TV screenwriter to dumb down the plays so we peasants can understand them. Maybe CTV could put them on after "Who Wants To Be A Millionaire?" with big name actors and actresses playing the lead roles. With any luck at all they will be on a cultural level with "The Simpsons" or "Buffy, The Vampire Slayer" or some other fine dramatic presentation.

We could run "MacFrasier" this Sunday night. Kelsey already has the part of the murderous Scot. Can't you see the three witches being played by the Golden Girls with Estelle Getty as the fourth witch visiting from Sicily?

First Witch: When shall we three meet again in thunder, lightning, or in rain?

Ma: Why do we always have to meet in the pouring rain? We can't meet when the sun is shining? My rheumatism is driving me crazy. Back in Sicily ...

First Witch: Will you cut the Sicily crap, Ma? We're trying to set up a meeting here. How be we meet on the heath when the hurly-burly's done?

Second Witch: When the "'what'" is done? We didn't have hurley-burley's back in St. Olaf, Dorothy.

First Witch: You didn't have indoor plumbing in St. Olaf, Rose?

I'm sure we can find a spot for the rest of the cast of "Frasier" in the show. Although, I'm not so sure about Eddie the dog. Dogs are notoriously unreliable in Shakespearean plays. Whenever they find a tree or a Styrofoam castle, they — well you know what would happen.

The hardest role to fill will be Lady Macbeth. She was a cold, calculating harpy with a razor-sharp tongue. I was going to suggest Sheila Copps, but I think I'll give it to the lady who was standing behind me in the supermarket line when my ATM card wouldn't work.

Why don't we get a day off for Shakespeare's birthday?

Shakespeare — a one-man job creation marvel

Yesterday was Bill Shakespeare's birthday and I'll bet not more than a half dozen of you sent him a card, or for that matter even celebrated the event with an Elizabethan dinner of chips and eels. (Eels were very big in the restaurants of late 1500s. In fact, the tasty dish was popular in England right up until 1989 when Margaret Thatcher invented the light bulb. People finally took a good look at what they were eating and headed right for the john. But what can you expect from folks who drink warm beer?)

I'm sure it came as no surprise to Bill that everyone forgot his birthday. We great authors are used to it. When I turned fifty all kinds of gentle folk showed up with quarts of Geritol and other insulting gifts, but after I started writing — nothing. Not that Bill and I are on the same level as writers — after all, I don't remember reading about him grinding out a column every week, but he was fairly good.

In my copy of *Bartlett's Familiar Quotations*, sixty-four pages are filled with excerpts from his plays and sonnets (a sonnet is any poem that doesn't start with *"Roses are red, Violets are blue"*). Those sixty-four pages are sacrilege when you realise that Bartlett only devoted two lines to the works of Woody Allen, who is without question the greatest author, philosopher, and youth worker of our generation.

I suppose I better add Stevie Leacock to our group of literary geniuses, not because he quite fits in with Bill, Woody, and me, but I don't need the Leacock Board of Directors on my back. I'm probably in enough trouble in Orillia after insulting the council last week. Fortunately, they are slow readers. By the time they figure out what I said, request a staff report from Ian Brown, the city manager, and hold another public meeting, I'll be on the old codgers' pension and living in the cottage some kind reader suggested the city build for me.

What really scares me is that once I move in, the council will sell the land around me to Canada Packers and build a bologna factory.

But Shakespeare's works will be remembered forever, not for the quality of his writings, or his insight into the human condition. Bill Shakespeare will be remembered as the man who single-handedly started the greatest job creation programme in history.

For 500 years, universities have had to pump out English teachers and professors by the truckload just to pound his plays into the heads of us dunderheads, who have no idea what the man was talking about.

I defy anyone to say that he or she would have understood one word of his works without a team of English Lit specialists on hand to interpret the man's scribbling.

For instance, we all use that great line from Macbeth — "Eye of newt, and toe of frog, wool of bat, and tongue of dog" — at least once a day. But do you have any idea what it means? Of course you don't. I had to phone the English department at Park Street Collegiate. (I called the schools in Barrie, but they are not as advanced scholastically. They are still working on *The Complete Works of Doctor Seuss*.) According to the teachers at Park, it's a recipe for chowder that Lady Macbeth served whenever her guests were into the booze and wouldn't leave. Just as a matter of interest, Lady Macbeth's first name was never mentioned in the play. I did a bit of research. It was Beulah.

For a man who did so much writing, it is remarkable that he ever sold anything. His language is incomprehensible and not only that, it's hard to understand. There's a line in *Othello*, "On horror's head horrors accumulate"; wouldn't it have been more to the point for him to say, "Holy Moses, Mary, what did the hairdresser do to your hair?"

We can excuse Bill's choice of words because he was born 435 years ago and did not have the advantages of a good education — like the latest one being designed by the Ontario Government. I can just imagine what scholars in the year 2435 will say when they try to read *Romeo and Juliet* after Snobelin, Johnson, and Janet Ecker get through with it.

What will future scholars do with those wonderfully romantic words of the fair Juliet?

"Good night, good night! Parting is such sweet sorrow,
That I shall say good night till it be morrow."

I can hear it now after their new curriculum:

"So I'll like, aah, see you around, Romeo. Now stop your blubbering and take off before my old man wakes up and runs his sabre through your doubloons."

Now I hate to criticize the work of my fellow critics, but this is carrying literary nosiness too far.

"Snoop" Foster puts literary world in a dither

Well I guess you all heard the shocking news by now — Anne of Green Gables was gay. Apparently our little Anne had relationships with at least three women. Interestingly enough, none of these affairs are in Lucy Maud Montgomery's books about Canada's carrot-topped heroine. A professor at the Royal Military College in Kingston discovered them by reading between the lines.

Now if Jane Stewart or Ernie Eaves told me this stuff I might have a few questions, but the woman who found this surprising bit of information about Anne's sexual preference is a professor of a well-known institution of learning.

I'm afraid I'm not all that bright. I can understand historians discovering that Caesar was a bed-wetter in some old scroll, or that Richard the lion-hearted wore pantyhose under his armour that was then woven into a tapestry found on a wall in an abandoned castle. But how can someone discover seedy affairs in works of fiction after the books have been on a library shelf for fifty years, and these little escapades aren't in there? What's to stop some unscrupulous writer from simply making up some trashy peccadillo and ruining a literary treasure?

What if some low-life scoundrel was to suggest that Zena Pepperleigh and Peter Pupkin were never married in *Sunshine Sketches of a Little Town* and lived in sin in one of those enchanted little houses on the hillside in the newer section of town? Orillia would never survive the scandal. We'd have to close the Leacock Home and all move to the Godless community of Barrie where that sort of thing goes on every day.

On the other hand, this could blossom into a whole new career for a money-grubbing little weasel like me — writing hitherto unknown scandals about fictitious characters — especially when the author has gone on to that great publishing house in the sky and can't sue me. Can't you see it all now in the *National Enquirer*?

JESSICA FLETCHER FOUND IN LOVE NEST WITH HERCULE POIROT

Literary busybody James Foster announced today that Cabot Cove mystery writer J. D. Fletcher has been involved in a long-term relationship with Belgian crime-fighter Hercule Poirot. Foster discovered the affair on page 62 of *The Case of the Missing Garter*. Collette Croissant, a chambermaid working the honeymoon suite at the Brussels's Holiday Inn, reported finding a pair of spats and what appears to be waxed nose hairs in Ms. Fletcher's bed. The disclosure came as quite a shock to Poirot fans. They thought the dapper sleuth was as queer as a three-dollar bill.

SUPERMAN — SUPER DUPE!

"Snoop" Foster made another outrageous statement today that has the publishing world in a dither. According to the mealy-mouth scandalmonger, *Daily Planet* reporter and long-time girlfriend of Krypton man of steel Superman, Lois Lane was found in a romantic tête-à-tête with Saxon do-gooder Robin Hood in a tree house in Sherwood Forest. Evidently, a disgruntled library employee scheduled for layoff as a result of Tory budget cuts had filed the Hood novel in the comic book section. Lois just slipped out of one book and slid between the covers of the other. This is not the first time that Ms. Lane has been found in questionable circumstances. Her "Night in the Bat Cave" series almost ruined the reputation of millionaire Bruce Wayne. Lane apparently has quite a thing for men in tights. At one time, the feisty journalist petitioned the American Library of Congress to have DC

Comics stored next to the Ballet Dance section. Fellow *Daily Planet* staffer Clark Kent was unavailable for comment.

WHAT TIME WILL YOU BE HOLME, SHERLOCK, WHINES WATSON?

All's not well that ends well in the Baker Street love nest of Britain's most famous detective and his long-time companion Dr. John Watson. According to Holmes' nemesis Professor Moriarty the couple have been publicly squabbling for weeks and were even ejected from Westminster Abbey when one of their frequent catfights threatened to ruin the wedding of Sir Nigel FitzGibbon-FitzHugh and socialite Lady Jane Backwater. The Archbishop himself tossed the two old pouffes out into the street. Apparently, Holmes had been seen in the company of Alfred J. Prinsmettle, a boy soprano, on a number of occasions.

You can see how this sort of thing could ruin the public's perception of the heroes and heroines of our favourite books. As readers, we must demand that government put a stop to it. Myself, I have a real problem with the article about Anne's gay tendencies. In a column last year, I accused her of having an affair with a P.E.I. lobster. Now no one will know who to believe.

We helpers never get any credit.

Great Watsons of the world overlooked

Have you ever wondered how Dr. John Watson must have felt when Alexander Graham Bell was given all the credit for inventing the telephone, knowing full well that most of the glory should have gone to him? Hardly anyone remembers that it was John, not Alec, who heard the phone ring, picked it up, and bought two tickets to the Shrine Circus.

It has ever been thus. Society has always honoured the inventor, never his assistant. The man who works long hours, often at minimum wage, is quickly forgotten when the awards are handed out.

No one is rushing out to buy shares in Watson Canada or pumping quarters into a Watson payphone to listen to a machine tell them to press 1 if they want service in English, 2 for service in French, and 3 if they would like to request a particular radio station to listen to while they are on hold until the next Tuesday.

How many remember, or have even heard of, Cedric Watson, Thomas Edison's helper? When Tom said, "Pick up that wire and tell me what you feel." It was Cedric who grabbed it and said, "Nothing." Nor did anyone record Edison's next words, "Well don't touch the one beside it. It's carrying 50,000 volts."

Of course, we all are familiar with Frederick Banting and Charles Best who discovered insulin. But where on the historical plaques honouring these two distinguished gentlemen do we see the name of their aged assistant Cyril Watson who sat on the needle?

History is filled with many more examples of these unfortunate oversights. Well, I suppose it really isn't, because we have no way of knowing that there ever was an assistant who was overshot. What about that great Norwegian Lars Watson who toiled alongside Peers Husqvarna perfecting the chainsaw? It was Lars, not Pers, who worked all week trying to cut down a Douglas fir tree. It was Lars, a week later when Husqvarna went to see what was keeping him and pulled the cord to start it, said, "What's that noise?"

Joseph Armand Bombardier is world-famous for inventing the first successful snowmobile. His company has branched out into every conceivable form of transportation from jet planes to streetcars. But I don't see anyone running out to buy a Jean-Pierre Watson snow machine or a Watson 747 named after Jean, the Watson who was lying under the snowmobile waxing the ski when Joe started it up.

Yes, there has always been a helper, a friend, or some poor soul, who happened to be walking by minding his or her own business, who contributed to every great discovery and was forgotten. (Oddly enough, they have all been named Watson — quite remarkable when you think about it.)

Yet, they never received international acclaim. No books were ever written about them. No movies of the life and loves of a Watson starring Don Ameche or Charlton Heston ever graced the silver screen. They are our unsung heroes and have been lost to history. There are no fig cookies named after Percy Watson, but it was Percy who was climbing the apple tree to get a better look into the bedroom of Miss Penelope Simms and knocked an apple down on the balding head of Sir Isaac Newton. Newton took all the credit for the discovery of the Law of Gravity, yet, without the clumsiness and voyeurism of Percy Watson, the Law would never have been passed and we'd all be lying on the ground hanging on for dear life.

We all understand how this happens. It isn't anyone's fault. That is one of the vicissitudes (I don't know what it means either) of life. However, one man must never be forgotten. There is one man to whom the world owes so much: Sir Angus Watson. It was Sir Angus who was instrumental in inventing that fine musical instrument we hear in the better concert halls today. Yes, my friends, I'm talking about the bagpipe. Although all the glory for the invention of this most intricate and melodic instrument was bestowed on Wild William Wallace many centuries ago, it was Sir Angus who really deserves the fame. Granted the world's first bagpipe crafted from his wife's tartan knitting bag and some drainpipes he found in his basement never worked. Wild Bill blew and blew for hours on end, yet he never produced one sound.

It was Sir Angus Watson who thought to stick in a cat.

The older I get, the more I'm inclined to believe that everything we were taught in history class is B.S.

Pilgrims, natives dine light and watch the game

Last Thursday was Thanksgiving Day in the U.S., a day set aside by George Washington to thank the Lord for allowing them to carry guns and shoot their next-door neighbour.

Americans have far more to be thankful for than we, their poor northern cousins. For one thing they can be thankful that Congress had the brains to hold their Thanksgiving on a Thursday giving them a four-day weekend.

The Americans invented Thanksgiving Day (and apparently everything else) to celebrate the fall harvest in 1641, and to give the Pilgrims an excuse to goof off for a day and watch the NFL games on TV. In the spirit of Christian fellowship, they also invited a few of the local Native Americans to join them for a feast.

I just happened to be going through Sharon's cosmetic drawer and found a tape of that first dinner. It was held at the spacious log cabin of Deacon Smith.

John Smith: Good afternoon, folks, and welcome to Plymouth Rock. I'm John Smith, thee can call me Jack. This is the little woman,

Felicity, and here are the kids, Obadiah, Joshua, Silas, Ezekiel, Sara, Purity, Patience, Prudence, and the twins, Heckle and Jeckle. Obadiah, get thy hand out of there. To my right is Elder Merriweather and his homely wife, Chastity. They have no children. To my left, Elder Goodbody and his missus, Charity, they have several. The rest of the settlement will be along for dinner right after the half time show. And now, thee are?

Running Deer: To be honest, I'm a little embarrassed. When you invited us to come over, I thought we were just going to play cards and watch the game. The wife could have whipped up some pemmican. Oh, I'm sorry, I'm Running Deer and this is the bride, Sparkling Waters.

Sparkling Waters: I wish you had let us know about the dinner, Felicity, and that all these other folks were coming. I could have at least brought a salad or something, maybe a zucchini casserole. It was a great year for zucchinis I've got them coming out my ...

Running Deer: I'm sure you have, my love. Oh, Jack, I brought along twenty-four skins of fermented moose milk. I thought we could sip away at it while we watch the game. I see by the way Elder Merriweather is dipping into it I should have fermented another moose.

John Smith: Bless thee, neighbour. We pilgrims are teetotallers usually — unless someone else is buying. Merriweather, don't use thy hands; I'll get thee a pewter mug.

Sparkling Waters: So what's for dinner, Felicity? Something light I hope. We had a buffalo for lunch.

Felicity: Turnip.

Sparkling Waters: Turnip. Turnip and what?

Felicity: Just turnip. That's the only thing we planted that came up.

Sparkling Waters: Turnips aren't food, Felicity. Turnips are for bowling or throwing at Iroquois. Don't you have any meat?

Felicity: John went out to shoot something but he's not very good at it. All he managed to do was wing Elder Cromwell.

Sparkling Waters: Well, don't you fret, dear. We can come up with something. Run, be a deer and shoot us a few turkeys, and maybe a partridge or something as a side dish. Oh, there are some blueberries in the freezer — under the bear steaks. Bring the bag marked "July 1640".

Running Deer: Can it wait, Sparky, the Washington Redskins are on the 10-yard line. Somehow I have the feeling that this will be the last time the Indians will win anything around here for a long time.

John Smith: Whilst thee are up, Running Deer, could thee bring back some of those roasted chestnuts that thy people make and some of that popcorn. That would be nice. We planted a box last spring, but it didn't come up. Just some things that look like rows and rows of yellow teeth.

Elder Merriweather: Oh, and we're getting a little low on the moose milk there, Cochise. Better bring a few more jugs. Do thee have any of those tobacco leaves thee gave to Wally Raleigh? I've been thinking of rolling them up in old newspapers and selling them to those dumb Canadians as health food.

Running Deer: Let's see, I better write all this down — a few turkeys, some partridge, blueberries, more booze, and some tobacco. Is that all?

Elder Goodbody: That's all for now. If we think of anything we'll let thee know.

Sparkling Waters: Hold on Run, I'll come with you to help you carry it all.

Elder Merriweather: Nice folks!

John Smith: They certainly are. Let's wait until after dinner to tell them we're taking their land to build a shopping mall.

Quite frankly, if I were going to build my own pyramid I'd put in a beer fridge!

Getting ready for the Great Beyond

I guess you've heard by now, French archaeologists have discovered another tomb in Egypt.

They found it back on March 25th. I was going to shout, "STOP THE PRESSES," but seeing as how it has been missing for 4,000 years, I figured another week or two wouldn't make much difference.

The ancient Egyptians have always fascinated me. For one thing they were kind of funny looking. I'm sure you've seen photographs of them. They had big eyes and their heads were on sideways. In fact they don't look unlike those aliens the Americans were supposed to have found near Roswell, New Mexico — only taller.

The pyramid belonged to Queen Ankh-sn-Pepi who was the wife of King Pepi the wunth. The Egyptians had some strange burial customs. They would often bury gold, jewels, and assorted other goodies like food, just in case the late queen felt a little gaunt on her way to the Great Beyond. Apparently, it wasn't unknown to throw in the odd slave to keep her company on the trip, which was one reason why Mutual of Cairo considered slaves a poor risk, and they rarely had insurance agents knocking on their door at dinnertime.

I was excited by the discovery, of course, but it started me thinking about what I would want to take with me when I go. Not that I'm planning on leaving in the next twenty minutes, but sometime in the third millennium I imagine someone will shoot me and I should really have a list ready. (I thought about being cryogenically frozen in case they can bring me back, but I've got a head cold now and it's 40°F. If I were frozen, my tomb would have to be wall-to-wall Dristan.)

I think I would like to take my beer label collection. I started it about three years ago when I bought a bottle of Bishop's Finger English beer at the liquor store. My wife thought it was a stupid idea because I'm great for starting projects I will never finish. But I fooled her this time. Already I have — well, just one label actually, but a good collection takes time.

I have a ballpoint pen with a girl in a bathing suit inside. When I turn the pen upside down her bathing suit disappears. I have never really seen what's under her suit. Whenever it falls off, she's upside down and if I bend over to look, I get dizzy and fall down. But I would like to take that with me. When some archaeologists discover me 3,000 years from now, I want them to know that I was a classy guy who was interested in art.

There's a set of barbells down in the basement that I guess I better take along. I never used them when I was alive, but you never know when they might come in handy. If nothing else, they will give the pallbearers a hernia. At least they'll remember me when I'm gone.

I have a book I borrowed from Pete McGarvey about three years ago. I'm too embarrassed to give it back to him now, so I'll just take it with me. While I'm at it, I'll pack one of my own books. I wrote one called "My Sexual Adventures and Other Failures." No publisher will publish it in this world; maybe I can find a sucker in the next.

I have a letter from Sophia Loren that I want to have with me. Well, it isn't exactly from Sophia, it's a court order saying I can't send her any more pictures of me barenaked and if I'm seen within a quarter of a mile of her, I'm to be shot on sight.

I have three or four pairs of pants that I got for Christmas over the years. They were all too small, and I said, "Don't take them back, I'm going on a diet." At one time I couldn't button them. Now I can't even get my foot down the leg holes. If I don't eat for 300 or 400 years,

I'm sure to drop an inch or two off the old waistline. I can hear the archaeologists now: "He's one goofy looking mummy, but don't his pants fit well?"

*It's amazing how little they teach these days about the War of 1812 —
or Barry Manilow's nose either.*

A Canadian heroine heads for the States

Well, I guess you heard the sad news. The Americans bought Laura
Secord Inc. Incidentally, that picture of Laura on the new boxes of
chocolates is not the same woman that was in my Grade 9 history
book. I suspect Laura may have had a face-lift, and maybe a nose job
or two, sometime over the past 187 years.

It's bad enough that the Yanks own everything else up here, but
now they control the rights to Canada's greatest heroine. Within a
year they will pull their usual stunt and rewrite the history books.
Suddenly our Laura will become an American patriot. Her exploits
during the War of 1812 will be cleverly Americanized by Stephen
Sondheim and turned into a Broadway musical. I can see the
reviews now.

Hello Laura starring Madonna. The heart-warming story of Laura
Secord, a young single mother raising her little adopted multi-
coloured family (six singing and dancing moppets) on the Niagara
Frontier, wowed the audience last night. Her wise-cracking twin sister,
Martha (Whitney Houston), was her usual self, breaking a number of

chandeliers and wine goblets as she shrieked out a number of hit songs from Stephen's newest and greatest musical.

The play opened as Martha is introducing Laura to Sir Isaac Brock (Barry Manilow) and they fall in love. In the end she has to betray him to save the United States from being taken over by his crack-team of Canadian magazine publishers. The Americans are worried that *Maclean's* will run a centrefold of Sheila Copps and put *Playboy* out of business.

Brock is killed at the end of the first act when he looks over Niagara Falls and the weight of his nose drags him into the Gorge. His schnozz (which you have to admit is pretty big even in this day of nuclear warheads) is later found floating in Lake Ontario and is now a children's waterslide at Fort Erie. As he floats down the river, we hear him sing that hauntingly beautiful love song "Nobody Nose the Troubles I've Seen." When he is sucked into the whirlpool, the audience breathes a sigh of relief.

Laura is devastated with grief and threatens to leap into the river until Whitney sings the lovely "Second Hand Nose" and Laura decides to eat a box of chocolates instead — especially the ones shaped like Karl Malden's beak. Heart-broken, Laura builds a huge statue of Sir Isaac on Queenston Heights overlooking the battlefield. On a clear day, his nose can be seen in Rochester, New York. (My wife says that I have a lot of nerve talking about Barry Manilow with the big honker I have stuck in the middle of my face — point well taken — heh heh did you get that? Point well taken? Oh never mind.)

Never one to rest on her laurels, which by the way are getting to be a fair size after eating all those chocolates, Laura decides to join the American army as a mess hall entertainer where she travels from camp to camp and meets Jim Bowie played by Leonardo DiCaprio. This is a stretch of the imagination since Leo looks to me like a guy who should be walking around with a ponytail and a fan on Fashion TV. Instead of carrying a Bowie knife, he should be packing a set of pinking shears. The two young lovers have a torrid affair behind the Wax Museum and decide to rent the honeymoon suite at the Fallsview Hotel since it's March and they're still on the off-season rates.

Unfortunately, the maid service leaves a chocolate on their pillows, which Laura promptly eats. Suddenly, she realises that she has a serious chocolate addiction and highjacks the linen cart carrying all the goodies. She stows enough shampoo and conditioner in her duffel bag to set up her own drugstore.

Eventually her face breaks out from all that chocolate. And as so often happens, her laurels spread until she can't sit on a buggy seat without hanging over both sides. Bowie finally tires of watching her eat and hitches a ride to Texas where he dies at the Alamo and not a moment too soon.

The show ends with everybody singing and Whitney trying to pry Laura out of the Jacuzzi.

You see what I mean. The Americans will ruin another Canadian company. But maybe more important, they will ruin Laura. We have to stop this erosion of our economy and our heroes by the Americans. I think that right after lunch tomorrow we should end this economic invasion by the Americans and send our troops across the border to burn Washington to the ground. We did it in the War of 1812. We can do it again.

Unfortunately, as your leader, I will have to stay behind and plan. But I want you to know that no matter what happens to you, I'll be with you in spirit. If by any chance you do get there and after beating you up, they send you home, would you mind picking me up a bottle of sour mash whisky at the duty-free shop — and a small box of Laura Secord chocolates?

This column was written to calm the fears of readers about the end of the world coming at midnight, December 31, 1999.

This prognosticator's vision slightly askew

It seems unbelievable to us visionaries that the prognostications of Michel de Nostradame, a 14th century astrologer and physician, are still being discussed in 1999, while the ravings of his contemporary, Johannes Nostrajamus are almost forgotten.

As Canada moves into the next millennium it is imperative that we take the time to study the writings of and marvel at the accuracy of his many predictions.

Whether Nostradame was divinely inspired to jot down his visions or just in the habit of sniffing airplane glue is unclear. Nostrajamus, on the other hand, is thought to have been heavily into substance abuse and the study of bird entrails. Let us look at a few of his prophecies and see just how many came true. Fortunately, a number of his scrolls were found recently in an old brandy cask in a Parisian wine shop. In the interest of science, I have translated them for you.

I, Johannes Nostrajamus, have seen the future and after I take my empties back, will take goose in hand and write down my auguries. (The scribbling seems to be somewhat blurred at this point and is barely legible. However, having studied penmanship under the guidance of my medical practitioner, I believe I have figured it out.)

MY VISION
(or hallucination, the French expression "Omigod, Je pense je am going to jettez mon cookies" can mean either.)

I see a day when a scientist will no longer have to look for bird entrails to prognosticate. They will come wrapped in little paper bags inside a turkey's bum. It will be the greatest boon to science since a falling apple gave Sir Isaac Newton a massive concussion.

I see a Scotsperson who will invent a voice machine that will enable a person far, far away to wake another in the dead of night to ask, "Is this the Couchiching Inn?" It will be a wondrous device and whole families will be able to buy accident insurance and vacuum cleaners right in the middle of their dinner. (Nostrajamus is referring, of course, to Benjamin Franklin who managed to send a kite up in an electrical storm and burn the bloomers off his wife, Fanny.)

I see a motion picture box. It shall be called "Le boite d'idiote." And every evening a great leader shall interview guests in leather or little attire who will confess that they are living with one lover, running around with a second, sleeping with a third, and having an affair with a fourth, yet all the time love the first one's grandmother. The programme shall be called "Pure Trash." Low-lifes by the millions shall tune in lest their spouse or daughter be on that night. (Historians believe that Nostrajamus may have seen a vision of "The National" with Peter Mansbridge.)

The powers that shall be will run what they will call "Christmas Specials" on the box, year after year after year, until the common man will crack and go looking for a Scrooge or Rudolph or fat person named Santa and bludgeon them unto death. Under the enlightened justice system of the time, shall they be imprisoned all day and forced to write, "I shall not bludgeon someone to death" no less than 100 times on a blackboard.

I see a man from the land of the eternal snows who shall be called The Harris who will destroyeth a whole province. Mercifully, shall he be hit with a nine-iron and institutionalized. (There is much debate as to whom Nostrajamus is referring. Although it is unlikely that it is our Harris, since he has closed most of the institutions and there are no institutions left to institutionalize him therein.)

A man shall invent a horseless carriage that shall run a thousand miles on a cupful of liquid called petrol or gasoline. It will be a most wondrous device until the petroleum companies jack the price up to $350 an ounce — $400 on the weekends. And the Feds shall do nothing, as usual, but go on a junket and vote themselves another raise. Lo, the people shall have had enough and shall they rise up and cast out the Liberals and the Conservatives and the Old Geezers' Party and the Seperatistes, and the other party whose name escapes me for the moment. They shall see the light and appoint a new leader to rule over all, responsible to no one. And he shall be from a small city in a place called Simcoe County and his name shall be Fos—

Here the writing becomes illegible as if the prognosticator has fallen face down and splattered his big nose all over the parchment.

IN THE EVENT THAT THE WORLD DISINTEGRATES AT 11:59 P.M., DECEMBER 31, PLEASE CHECK NEXT WEEK'S COLUMN FOR FURTHER INSTRUCTIONS!

More historical "facts" that need investigation.

History may just be guys one-upping each other

Have you ever wondered if all those interesting historical stories we were taught in school were true, or could some of them be figments of some early bozo's imagination?

Do you really believe King Harold got nailed in the eye with an arrow at the Battle of Hastings? Maybe he just had a sty and died while trying to lance it with a meat fork?

Some of those stories seem a trifle far-fetched to me now. There was supposed to be a King Arthur back in 600 AD — but was there? And if there was, did Art actually build a Round Table? Why wouldn't he just buy one from Leon's? He wouldn't have had to pay a cent until 601?

I'm not so sure an Italian artist named Michelangelo painted the ceiling of the Sistine Chapel either. I think he and the Pope just picked up some fancy wallpaper at an "end of the line" clearance sale at McPhee Paint and Wallpaper and stuck it on the roof. The history books say Mike took thirty years to finish the job. That's possible, but is thirty years really an abnormally long time when there's a union decorator involved and he's being paid by the hour? It took me six months to paper the bathroom. I couldn't get the stuff to stick on the wall. I can imagine how long poor Mike must have taken to paper a ceiling. And he probably wasn't using the pre-pasted stuff that we use and find curled up on the floor in the morning.

I'm beginning to have serious doubts about things we were taught in school — especially when I know the historians were men and the tales were passed down around campfires by a bunch of guys trying to one-up each other.

I'm sure you, dear reader, have noticed that even the most boring and trivial of stories tend to get embellished just a tad when the hour gets late and someone opens another jug. That perch that measured slightly less than the worm you were using for bait has strangely grown to be a Great White over the years, and now you distinctly remember a deep-sea diving suit and a harpoon being involved.

It is amazing when you think about it, how faulty our minds can be about things in the past. To think your recollection of an afternoon fishing from a rowboat could be so fuzzy that you completely forgot you were cruising off New Guinea in a Chinese junk when the monster struck.

History is much the same. We don't know whether to believe it all or not. Was there really a Julius Caesar and did he fool around with Cleopatra on a barge? Or did Bill Shakespeare make the two of them up?

Did a Carthaginian general named Hannibal march a troop of elephants across the Alps? If he was so great, why didn't someone name a car after him like they did for Desoto and LaSalle? Where is this Carthage anyway? The only one I can find on my CAA map is in New York State. Surely Hannibal didn't march a herd of elephants along the New York State Thruway. If he did, they'd still be halfway to Schenectady. Plus, the tolls would have bankrupted him.

Now I know I'll get in trouble with the religious folks, but do you really believe Joshua levelled the walls of Jericho just by blowing a hot lick on a trumpet. I've heard a few pipers hit some pretty sour notes during the Scottish Festival in Couchiching Park, but I don't remember the washroom walls tumbling down. (Come to think of it, a dozen tents were flattened and Sam Champlain's hat blew off, so that's not a good example.)

The Jonah and the Whale story is a little suspect too. I think old Jonah was dangling a finger in the lake and a snapping turtle got him. He wasn't a hero. He just had a press agent with a good imagination.

I have my doubts about the day that King Harold croaked. It's a great story, but there was no one there from the media, so how do we know it really happened? If Dan Petkovsek from the New VR had been holding his video camera 6" from the end of Harry's beak, I might believe it. But even then I would want it confirmed by Bob McIntyre or someone from the *Packet*.

I hate to think what kids will be studying in the future about heroes and politicians of today. A buck says they won't be reading about Tom Long, Preston Mandrell, and Stockyard Day. My bet is History 101 in the year 3000 will be about Bill and Monica floating down the Nile on a barge.

I've heard of the Mile-High Club, but this is ridiculous.

Everyone wants to spice up his or her love life

I'm sure you've all heard or read about the young British couple that met on an American Airlines flight from Dallas to Manchester and decided to fly United instead.

It was obviously a case of lust at first sight. Of course, booze was involved, as it usually is, and from what I have gleaned from the news report, not a whole lot of brain cells.

Aside from all the publicity (their pictures were in every newspaper and TV channel from here to Rangoon), the fines ($5,200), and the fact they were both fired, can you imagine the conversation when they had to call home to tell their spouses?

"I say, ducks, I shall be a trifle late for tea. I've met a young lady who is a telecommunications executive and we've being going over her briefs."

"Nigel, old bean, I shan't be home for tiffin. There seems to have been a bit of a balls-up with the travel arrangements. Do be a dear and contact our barrister. Oh yes, would you ring up mommy and tell her my picture is going to be on the telly?"

According to newspaper reports, the incident added friction to their marriages. I wouldn't doubt that. I also wouldn't doubt it will be the only friction they will be getting in their marriages for years to come.

And yet, dear friends, in a way, we have to admire this carefree pair of star-crossed lovers. Haven't we all secretly wanted to do something wild and exciting? I know, I know, it's not socially acceptable and there is the marriage vows, the infidelity and all that to consider, but just imagine it was you up there at 20,000 feet and the opportunity arose. Granted most folks would have found a spot a little more private for their tryst, like a bench in the Eaton Centre, but how many of us haven't at one time or other wanted to throw caution to the winds and act on some wild impulse?

I know had it been Sophia Loren and I on that flight with two bottles of wine, port, and a bottle of cognac, poor Soph would have been hard pressed to keep her hands off of me — and who could blame her, really? She would have been all over me like dog hair on a blue suit. An opportunity like that would only come once in her lifetime.

Was this affair in the clouds really all that much different than Romeo and Juliet's little fling in Verona — other than the kids weren't married to someone else, were on the ground, and Romeo was wearing lime green tights? I think not. Therapist and marriage counsellors have long been saying there is no harm in a couple living out their little fantasies. (Our favourite is the one where I dress up like Lord Conrad Black and Sharon flies to London and buys another newspaper.)

In fact, acting out fantasies can be good for a stale marriage. I know a couple whose marriage was enriched immensely when the husband had just such a mad passionate affair. Except for the fact she now has the house, the car, the kids, and is married to someone else, while he lives alone in an abandoned fish hut, they still look back on the incident as the defining moment in their relationship.

I have always admired people who make friends easily. Obviously these two, Amanda and David, are particularly good at it.

Even in the halcyon days of my youth, I was unable to approach a young lady without spending hours in rehearsal just to say hello. Once I had overcome my fear of rejection and actually asked her out, it would take me six weeks to get up enough nerve to write her father for permission to hold her hand. Then it would be another month before I had the nerve to take off my gloves. By the time I felt comfortable enough in the romance to kiss her fingertips, she was married to someone else and had four kids.

But this couple seemed to be able to skip all that. If these two were ball players, they'd go right from spring training to the World Series.

I guess the thing that amazes me about the whole affair isn't that they fell madly and passionately in love on a jumbo jet, but that someone on board complained. They certainly had to be infinitely more entertaining than some of the in-flight movies they've been showing lately.

I have always been fascinated by advice to the lovelorn columns.

For 4,500 bucks I'll find you a man

This column is for the ladies. Men won't understand it. It has to do with interpersonal relationships and other things they won't have a clue about.

I read a fascinating article about Marriage Works, a husband-hunting service in New York that is available for a mere $9,600 U.S. For this piddling amount, Marilyn Graman, a Manhattan psychotherapist, will get a young lady ready for marriage.

She won't find her a husband, unfortunately, but she will put her client in a more receptive mind-set. (I would think a woman who just blew $9,600 isn't likely to have much of a mind to set.) What she will get however, is a six-month programme that includes a talk with an interior designer on how her living space may be inadvertently shutting out men.

Not only that, Marriage Works will send a consultant to her home and make her closet man-ready. I would imagine throwing out thirty pairs of shoes, four lime green bridesmaids dresses, and that life-size blow-up doll of Peter Mansbridge would help.

There is a trip to a bridal salon thrown in, and even question and answer sessions with real, live men on how to act like a goddess.

Finally, a woman has actually figured out what it is that we men want — a goddess. Not a goddess like Venus de Milo. She had no arms and her husband had to do the dishes.

The trouble is for $9,600 U.S. — that's $13,920 in good old Canadians loonies — the poor girl still doesn't have a man.

I can't let you ladies waste another dime on this stuff in hopes that someday you might stumble on some guy sleeping one off in the park and drag him to the altar. You need guarantees. Therefore, I have decided to open Little Jimmy's Dating Service to find you a man — or something fairly close to it.

This is not some get-rich-quick scheme to bilk you out of 13 grand — far from it. I can do it for $2,500 ($4,500 tops) — unless you insist on one who has a job and doesn't comb his sideburns over his bald spot, but we can discuss all those special requests during my fraud hearing. Please take a few moments to answer this simple questionnaire and drop it in to the *Packet* — along with a cheque for $2,500 — better make that $4,500.

NAME (yours — I already know mine)

AGE (I know I have no right to ask for such personal information. However it would be silly for me to send a young virile Brad Pitt-type to some old dolly in her 30s or 40s. That isn't what those women are looking for. They are searching for a mature gentleman. I'd go myself, but Sharon won't let me out after supper.)

HAVE YOU EVER BEEN MARRIED? (Again this may seem irrelevant, but if you've already worn out one man, I'm not sure you should get a shot at another. We mustn't be greedy — unless of course, you are willing to cough up a few more bucks.)

Perhaps the most important part of the stud application form is the following section: WHAT EXACTLY ARE YOU LOOKING FOR IN A MAN?

HEIGHT (Be honest, but bear in mind that a male's intelligence grows in inverse proportion to his height, i.e., Albert Einstein was a little runt about my size, while slower folks like politicians and circus geeks are much taller.)

WEIGHT (Most women prefer us pudgier gentlemen since we are rarely abducted by conniving divorcees. There are drawbacks, of course. One that comes to mind is taking a beefy chap to a beach. Far too often, he is surrounded by environmentalists, wetted down, and dragged back into the ocean. The second is they are often mistaken for sofas and re-upholstered.

DO YOU MIND A SOCIAL DRINKER? (A social drinker is a chap who consumes less than twelve beers or a quart of alcohol a day. A problem drinker is one who often wakes up naked in a strange city wearing roller blades and a pinwheel hat.)

DO YOU MIND A BED-WETTER? (A woman complained to Ann Landers that her new husband wets the bed. If she is going to be that picky, she doesn't deserve a husband. She should have bought a fern instead. This minor problem is a normal part of married life — unless of course he stands up while doing it.)

That's just about it for my dating service application. Oh, one other thing, if you want a guy who uses deodorant occasionally, it might cost you a few bucks extra.

Am I the only Canadian who thinks Céline is just a tad goofy?

Even animals invited to Céline's wedding

I don't know if you received your invitation to Céline Dion's latest wedding or not. It probably ended up with ours — on a shelf somewhere in the dead letter office at Canada Post, along with my invitation to be the centrefold in this month's *Cosmopolitan*, and some accessories I ordered from a Hong Kong honeymoon catalogue.

I wish I had been invited though; it sounded exciting. I've been to all kinds of weddings over the years, but never one with six Berber tents, jugglers, musicians, and camels.

I think it's nice to invite animals to a wedding. They never get invited anywhere.

A couple of years ago, a couple got married at the Orillia Fall Fair. They rode off in a goat cart. I don't think the goat was part of the ceremony. I wonder if they ever had a kid. (I know I used that same line after the wedding, but sophisticated humour like that is rare these days and should be used over and over until your life is threatened.)

Céline's big bash wasn't all that big for a Hollywood wedding. It was just an intimate, little family affair, with few hundred close friends, the animal trainers, and the entire cast of *Lawrence of Arabia*.

The tab was around $1.5 million U.S. (The bill for the wedding itself was only $1,400; the rest was to clean the rug after the camels pooped on it.)

Of course, it wasn't a real wedding. The happy couple just renewed their vows in case one or the other forgot the first set. I don't know if you've noticed, but quite often vows at a renewal ceremony are worded just a little differently than they were originally. The love, honour, and *obey* line is still in, but this time it's the *man* who has to say it.

In the case of Céline and her hubby, she's the one with the bucks, so René had to go along with it or he'd end up sitting on an ice floe in the St. Lawrence with nothing but his bedroom slippers and the toque on his tête.

If you haven't been following this latest turn in Céline's career, the Dion-Angélils are taking a five-year career hiatus to try to have a baby, or as one Montreal columnist put it — to practise their progenitive skills.

"Céline, what's avec all de fedders and mattress stuffings floating out your window dere? Avez-vous had une h'explosion?"

"Non, mama, René et moi practeesez notre skeels progeniteeve h'ontil hees eyes dey bug h'out."

I don't know much about French people or how they make babies, but if there's a camel involved there's going to be more than someone's career having a hiatus.

It's difficult enough for celebrities to lead a normal life, what with reporters following them around or hiding under their beds, but once the word gets out that they're throwing a big splash with jugglers, free booze, and live animals, every freeloader in town shows up.

That isn't much of a problem in Orillia. Most $1.5 million dollar weddings here hardly get mentioned in the *Packet* unless the bride buys an ad or the O.P.P. are called in to break up a fight.

I wonder what kind of eats they serve at million-dollar weddings. When Sharon and I got married, we passed around little cheese balls from M & Ms during the ceremony. (We didn't know you had to cook them, and they were frozen. The only person who made any money that day was Bob Carroll, my dentist.) Once the Rev said the "I do thee wed," everyone went out to McDonald's and drove by the take-out window with our horns blowing.

Céline and Renée are French, you know. I don't know what they had for snackies, but I imagine there was lot of poutine and patates

43

frites. I hope they didn't have escargot. There is nothing that will ruin a good wedding faster than the guy beside you eating escargot. If Bouchard ever takes off with Quebec, that's the only thing we can let him have for nothing — the damn snails.

But even though Céline didn't invite us to the wedding, we hold no hard feelings, and wish the two of them well as they spend the next five years practising their progenitive skills. One good thing about it, if Céline has headache, René can always hop on the camel and ride down to the Legion for a bière.

Sometimes my duties as a newspaper marriage counsellor become too demanding. So many lives to ruin and so little time.

Wife will indicate when the "zing" is gone

A few months ago, I read an excellent article, "Cues and Clues in the Mating Game." I can't remember where, but I know it wasn't in the *Orillia Packet and Times*. For the benefit of you folks in Midland and Collingwood, the *Packet* is the flagship of Conrad Black's newspaper empire. Our motto is "Yesterday's News Tomorrow." We pride ourselves on keeping on top of the rapidly changing events around the globe. Yesterday's headline for instance was "Japanese fleet seen off Pearl Harbour."

"Cues and Clues" was an excellent article on the present state of romance in our society. It occurred to me that as your marriage counsellor this might be an ideal time to start a two-part series on the latest trends in the game of love.

It is a well-known fact that even the most passionate of marriages begin to lose that old "zing" after forty or fifty years. I'm sure that even you have experienced a momentary lull in the excitement of your romance at some time or other. For the first while, couples can't get enough of each other. Life is just one mad whirl of desire and passion.

Eventually however, all couples grow out of the honeymoon stage (that's what we in the therapy game call those first few months when newlyweds can't keep their hands off each other).

The "I can hardly wait until tonight" becomes "Don't tell me it's July again," or "I don't know. I'll have to check the *TV Guide* first."

It happens to us all unfortunately. In the beginning, all you had to do was look at each other. Then it becomes the "Oh, oh, he has that look again. I'll pretend I don't see it and finish the laundry," and finally it's "Not again! I wonder if the police would believe he committed suicide by holding a pillow over his own face."

Some couples are able to make the zing last for years. I have known couples who were quite active into their 30s — although admittedly not all that many. Others, sadly, barely make it through the first night.

There are several signs that the spark has gone out of a marriage. Some are fairly obvious, like the exchange of gunfire on a regular basis. Another thing that suggests there may be problems is frequent visits by the local constabulary to break up a domestic disagreement, usually at the request of neighbours.

But a number of subtle, little signs are easily missed when assessing the state of a marriage and/or relationship.

For the male, there are a number of telltale hints to suggest your wife is not quite as thrilled with your romantic endeavours as she once was. For example, if, while you are making mad passionate love, your wife mentions the ceiling needs painting, that is considered a bad sign. If she actually gets up and starts putting on a primer, it may mean that you are not exactly Brad Pitt, and it's time for you to retire from connubial activities and join the Canadian Alliance.

If at the height of passion, your wife turns on the Martha Stewart show, because Martha is demonstrating a new recipe for cooking turkey, it might simply mean company is coming. On the other hand, it could be an indication that there is more than one turkey in the household and one of them isn't in the freezer.

Another bad sign is your wife going to bed wearing a sleep mask, and Dr. Denton pyjamas with the feet in them and a combination lock on the zipper. Unless you have a locksmith's home phone number scribbled on the headboard, try not to get your hopes up.

If your wife says, "Just a minute I have to go to the bathroom" and takes a book, that may be a sign. If she takes *Penthouse*, that's good. If she takes *War and Peace*, you might as well get up and finish raking last year's leaves.

Sometimes we sex therapists will advise a couple to act out their favourite fantasies in order to keep the passion alive. If those fantasies involve a pirate captain and a captured Spanish noble woman, it can be quite exciting. If however, a motorcycle and the local chapter of the Hell's Angels are part of the routine, you might want your doctor to schedule the two of you for a psychiatric assessment.

A common fantasy is to imagine your partner is a famous movie star. That can be quite fulfilling. Or it can be quite disturbing, particularly if your wife is addicted to Saturday morning cartoons. It is one thing to have her cry out "Oh, Cary." Shouting, "Oh, Popeye" is something else again.

Next week, we will explore the many signs you ladies might look for that suggest your paunchy, little Leonardo DiCaprio is wandering, or worse, rapidly approaching the geezer stage.

No irate phone calls about last week's column, so I'll risk another.

Read between the signs and lines of love

If you will remember (I know it's been a whole week but some folks can remember simple things for as long as a month before the stuff disappears), we were discussing a column I read entitled "Cues and Clues in the Mating Game," and the telltale signs that a relationship may be having problems. Last week I was telling the men what to look for. This week the discussion is strictly for you ladies.

There are a number of danger signs might lead a woman to believe that her beloved is sewing his wild oats in someone else's acreage. If he picks up a softball glove and says, "I think I'll go down to the park and shag a few flies with Harry," you might be a trifle suspicious. If however, he heads out the door with the old ball glove and it's the 12th of January and eleven o'clock at night, you might want to grab a Louisville Slugger baseball bat and follow him.

If he says he's going to drop down to the Legion for a beer, but splashes on aftershave and packs his pyjamas, that's a bad sign. If he splashes on aftershave and pops a Viagra, that's worse.

On the other hand if he is just not as attentive as he once was, the poor, old dear might be getting old, and can't keep up with you.

(You've known for years you should never have married a man ever so many years your senior.)

There are a few things to watch for — like forgetfulness during the romance thing. If you wake up and he is staring at you and appears confused, just say, "You were wonderful, dear," and he will roll over and not bother you for the rest of the night.

These are just a few helpful hints that will help you understand just where your marriage is in the grand scheme of things. But that is not what the article was about.

"Cues and Clues in the Mating Game" was about courtship and dating.

It was a one-page instruction manual on how to tell if that young girl in the halter top, or for you ladies, the tall, dark stud in the torn t-shirt with the bum out of his jeans, is coming on to you or not. There is nothing more embarrassing for a man to make a move on some young thing in a bar who is waving at him, only to find out that she had mistaken him for her Uncle Harry who is 82 years old and incontinent.

As I was telling a nurse who understands these things, "I'm not incontinent. I just keep peeing my pants all the time." That has nothing to do with the topic. I just hate to waste a good line like that. It's not exactly flattering for the young lady either to slink over to that young guy with his ball hat on backwards (a sure sign of mental retardation), only to find he thought she was his Grade 1 teacher, Old Lady Farnsworth.

That wraps up this lesson, with the exception of opening lines. If you, madam, would like to get chummy with that nice gentleman at the end of the bar, in the black leather biker jacket and the helmet with the horns sticking out the side, what are you going to say to him to show that you are interested in meeting him for stimulating conversation?

And you sir, what are you going to say to that young lady sitting alone at a table to show her that you are a gentleman and not after her for her body, which you just happened to notice measures 38-24-36 with legs that are shapely and go all the way to the ground?

There are several crackerjack pick-up lines I can suggest:

The ever popular, "What's a nice girl like you doing in a place like this?" is a great line. On the other hand, if the girl is leaning against a lamp post and she says, "working" you might want to consider heading to an all-night clinic for a penicillin shot.

"Hello, sailor, do you want to buy a girl a drink?" always worked well for ladies during the war. Although after their husbands came home from overseas, as Ricky Ricardo used to say, they had some "splaining" to do.

But if you are my age, there is one line that is guaranteed to work every time: "Will you come to my house and help me move my couch? I've thrown my back out again."

More advice to the lovelorn.

Little Jimmy will guide you to wedded bliss

I guess you were as shocked as I was to read that Darva and Rick Rockwell packed it in. They are the couple who met, wooed, and wed all in two hours on that fine intellectual TV show "Who Wants to Marry a Multi-Millionaire?"

Alas, I'm afraid their little love boat floundered on the storm-tossed Sea of Matrimony. It sank apparently before their marriage was even constipated. I shouldn't bring this up in a family newspaper, but Darva had to file her annulment. I'm sure that must have been very painful for the young bride.

The whole mess could have been avoided if she and Rick had taken the time to have a few pre-nuptial sessions with a clergyman instead of just checking into the bridal cabin at the Bide-a-Wee Inn and Family Resort.

Better yet, they should have coughed up a few bucks and registered at Little Jimmy's Marriage Preparation Weekend. This wonderful seminar is held several times a year at a bevy of seedy motels around the province. For just $500 (soap and towels extra), they could have joined with other lusty, young couples in a concentrated programme of study, advanced sexual techniques, and sage advice guaranteed to start them down the road to wedded bliss under the tutelage of an expert in such matters. After a fun-filled, yet informative, three days, the couples leave — often with the same person — with the knowledge of how to build a satisfying relationship that will last for weeks.

I have helped so many. I hate to boast, but it was my seminar that started Elizabeth Taylor off on her matrimonial adventures, not once, not twice, but nine successful times. Space (and the fact that you aren't paying for this) doesn't allow me to delve too deeply into most modern marriage problems, but I shall mention a few.

The single most important cause of marriage breakdown today (other than nocturnal intestinal gas) is poor communication — particularly for men. Men are bozos. We all know that, but it isn't their lack of intelligence that is the problem. Men are born with under-developed listening genes. The message is lost in the mass of scientific and highly technical information that the average man deals with every day.

What he needs to learn is my secret to marital communication. To be more specific, it is not how well he listens, but how he can appear to be spellbound by a woman's words while his mind is off working on a more complicated problem like, what would have happened if Jennifer Lopez had sneezed while wearing her Emmy Award dress? The secret is "mumble."

Too often, the novice makes the dreadful mistake of actually appearing to agree with whatever his partner is saying instead of simply muttering "uh, huh" or "mmm hmmm" like we older, experienced chaps. In his desire to please, he will often blurt out "yes" without having the faintest idea what he just blurted "yes" to. Twenty minutes later, he's standing in a paint store, while his wife thumbs through colour charts for just the right shade of green to match the new furniture that he didn't know he agreed they were buying. Worse, he vaguely recalls his missus saying something about him getting off his bum to do the painting. He remembers agreeing to paint *someday*, but he didn't realize that that *someday* meant *today*.

On Saturday afternoon, the couples will learn several advanced lovemaking techniques, and the men will be taught why a punch on the arm is no longer considered foreplay. Reasons why enjoying two beers and a pepperoni sandwich before bedtime will rarely inflame a bride's passion will also be discussed.

The seminar is certainly not just male oriented. There are hundreds of helpful suggestions to help future wives appreciate the joy of having a man around the house. She will learn why opening a beer for her beloved is the sweetest, simple, little display of love and affection that will keep him happy — until he snaps his fingers for another.

The Sunday Morning Sunrise Session starts at 6:30 for the ladies, while the men catch up on some much-needed shuteye. After all, they worked all week. A pre-programmed video will explain the medical reasons why men should never scrub toilets. There will also be a discussion of the alarming statistics connecting male prostate problems to household vacuum cleaners. A husband would be only be too happy to help with what is so obviously women's work, but do you girls really want to put that loveable slob lying on the couch in danger?

I hate to complain, but I have been snapping my fingers for the last ten minutes. Perhaps while getting me a beer, someone in this house should be thinking about a refresher course at Little Jimmy's Marriage Preparation Weekend.

It's amazing what you can learn from a newspaper if that's all you have to read in the bathroom.

Wedding smarts — a contradiction in terms

The other day I took one of those newspaper quizzes on wedding smarts. (I have a friend who is now going through his fourth divorce who tells me that the words "wedding" and "smarts" should never be used in the same sentence. To avoid any more trouble with women, he has hired a student to pour ice water down his pants any time he starts chatting to a lady.)

But back to the quiz.

Number one on the list of questions was "What is considered bad luck for any wedding?" The answers were the usual dumb superstitions that I had never heard before.

1. The bride buying her ring on a Friday. (I'm so stupid; I thought the groom bought it.)

2. The couple marries on the bride's birthday. (I can think of a good reason for not doing that. It's bad enough to forget her birthday, but to forget her birthday *and* your anniversary is the first step to sitting across from the missus on the "Jerry Springer Show.")

3. The bride marries in black shoes. (If that's all she's wearing, I

can see it being a problem, although it will make for an interesting picture in Joella's Cheers section in the *Packet*.)

4. The groom carries his wallet on his wedding day. (Now, I never realized that carrying cash was unlucky. Although, not having any money almost certainly guarantees that he won't stop off at the First Hotel for a few beers on his way from the church to the reception.)

There was another one about the bride's veil catching fire, but the rest were all pretty tame. Whoever wrote this test obviously has had no experience with wedding problems. I can give them a few more.

It is bad luck when the bride and groom are standing at the front of the church and a little kid walks up the aisle, tugs the groom's sleeve, and says, "Mommy wants to know what time you are coming home for dinner."

Another unlucky sign is the O.P.P. surrounding the building and shouting to the groom, "We have the building surrounded. Come out with your hands up." Or when the Rev asks, "Does anyone have any reason why these two should not get married?" and half the guests line up at the microphone with lists.

It's bad luck if the bride goes into hard labour during the ceremony.

It's bad luck if the groom and the best man are holding hands during the ceremony. It's not much better if the bride and the best man are holding hands behind the groom's back.

It's bad luck if the bride's agent calls on her cell phone and asks her if she can work a stag party later that night. It's even worse if she says, "Yes."

It's bad luck if the flower girl comes down with the mumps and the groom starts to swell up, and the part that's swelling isn't his face.

I'm sure there are more.

The next question on the quiz was "What is considered good luck for any wedding."

Apparently, it's good luck if the bride wears old underwear. I would think it's good luck if after paying for the wedding dress, the reception, and all the other incidentals that will add up to a few grand, the bride can even afford underwear.

It's good luck if the bride sees a dove, frog, goat, lizard, or a lamb. Are they going to a wedding or is this a trip to the Elmvale Zoo?

Now get this. It is considered good luck if the bride and groom don't bathe and the bride dances every dance at the reception. I would think that if neither has bathed and she is dancing all the time, the good luck would be if the rest of the guests don't stampede out the door, and the owner of the hall doesn't send them a bill for fumigating the place.

I have no idea who dreams up all these wedding superstitions. The only guy I ever heard of who really got lucky at his wedding was Prince Edward. His wife, Sophie, agreed to leave the obey line in the ceremony. Now that's the sign of a good wife and also ...

"What?"

I'm sorry, I have to go now, Sharon says I have to take out the garbage.

"Coming, my pet."

Some days, we can see just a bit too much of the stars.

Hair today — gone tomorrow

This is rather a delicate subject. You children may want to ask your parents to leave the room while you read this stuff.

You can imagine how shocked I was to see a front-page story in the *National Post* about Julia Roberts' underarm hair. It would have been bad enough to just mention it (or them, apparently there may be more than one), but they had the audacity to show a coloured photo of Julia with her arm up waving to her fans. At least it appears that it is Julia's underarm hair showing. It may be a squirrel or another one of God's furry creatures awakening from a long winter's nap.

The Star, not realizing what an important news item this was, relegated it to page two. What were they thinking?

Naturally, the reporter covering this newsworthy event interviewed a number of prominent women in the Toronto business and educational community. They were asked whether we should let this fashion faux-pas go this time and let her off with a written warning, or whether Julia should be taken to the marketplace and stoned.

One woman, although concerned that this might start a trend, was kind enough to suggest that Julia might be letting it grow for a part in an upcoming movie. That's quite possible; I understand that they are doing a remake of *King Kong* and the gorilla role is still up for grabs. According to my sources in Hollywood, it's a toss-up between Julia and Rin Tin Tin.

It is amazing what a tempest in a teapot this glimpse into the semi-private area of a major movie star has caused. There were comments everywhere from "gross" to "a fashion statement." Typical of the Toronto media, they didn't bother to send a news team to interview us folks in Simcoe County, the people who are on the cutting edge of Canadian haute couture. You'd think we were hillbillies for heaven's sake.

As the guru of fashion in Simcoe County (anyone who saw me Saturday at the liquor store wearing my shorts with the bum out and my one-size-fits-no-one beer shirt will understand why I have been chosen to represent the fashionable dressers in the area), I feel it necessary to add my 2 cents worth.

To start, I think Julia looks sexy. Although, I must admit that I am a little prejudice. Ever since I saw her in that wonderful movie *Pretty Woman*, I've been smitten by her beauty and innocence. Even as she stood on that Hollywood street corner dressed in a mini-skirt, scooped-necked blouse, thigh-high riding boots, with one leg up on a hydrant, her purity shone through.

Most people who saw the film thought she was playing the part of a hooker, but I could see that she was portraying a social worker struggling along on the 500 bucks a night she earned as a gentleman's companion.

But my feelings toward Julia — and why my wife made me take down the life-sized poster of her off the ceiling of our bedroom — are not important right now. What we need to discuss is whether underarm hair is acceptable in today's society or whether all women should be dipped in a tank of Nair every morning before they are allowed out on the street.

You might be surprised to learn that the clean-shaven look is not all that popular in several European countries. In some cultures, a woman's beauty is based on the number of braids she can put in her underarm hair and still get her arms down low enough to scratch.

Shaving is a subject that is very upsetting to women. It is one of the many things that ladies don't talk about in mixed company —

such as passing gas or why a person would be dumb enough to believe a Mike Harris TV commercial. The topic has been avoided for centuries. It was never mentioned in the historical records whether the great women of history started the day with a few slashes of the old Gillette, or whether their underarms and shanks were covered in hair or moss.

I saw a picture of Queen Elizabeth the Wunth, and she was the prime example of a girl who should have let her arm hair grow long — long enough so she could comb it over her face. Liz wasn't what you would call a pretty maiden. Instead of putting his cape over a puddle when Liz walked by, Sir Walter Raleigh could have done London a favour and thrown it over her head.

At this year's Oscar presentations, Whoopi Goldberg came out dressed as Queen Liz. I had nightmares for weeks. Now that I think of it, Whoopi is not what you would call a "looker" either.

We don't know if Marie Antoinette was clean-shaven, or Cleopatra, or for that matter Eve herself. After all, Adam would hardly be a good judge of feminine beauty having no one to compare her to. Whether body shaving was important back then or not, we don't know. But I don't remember Adam ever saying to his missus, "By the way, my pet, you better fire up the old Remington, the serpent has invited us over to the orchard for dinner."

I hope that clarifies the situation. Now if you don't mind I have to go and see what I can do about my nose hair. Some days, I just can't do anything with it.

This column is really for us old folks looking for a hobby.

Skateboarding for seniors

The other day I was walking through the park and saw a whole raft of kids leaning on shovels. Naturally, I assumed they were Georgian students training for a supervisor's job with the Orillia Works Department. But no, they were helping the Kiwanis Club build a skateboard thingy for the young 'uns.

Am I the only one in town upset over this? Why didn't they build a skateboard park for us seniors? Now I have no problem with kids sailing up and down a cement wall, but for another 50 grand they could have built one for us geezers — a little higher of course, say 30 or 40 feet? Well, it stands to reason that once a person reaches a certain age his or her senses become far more acute. Our natural agility ripens over the years. Seniors are far more athletic than children. Our skills and dexterity have been honed by three-quarters of a century of athletic challenges; the average senior, of say 80, is far more capable of handling a skateboard than some kid in goofy pants.

With our lightning fast reflexes, we could put those little nippers to shame. Why just this winter I was following Pete McGarvey down the Mississauga Street hill when he hit a patch of ice. I would be very surprised if a child of 19 or 20 could have ever pulled off a triple axel like Pete did before he hit that parking meter. (Back in January, parking meters were free. If it happened today, the meter person would have a $5.00 tag hanging on him before his nose hit the ground.)

I gave him a 9.9, stepped over him, and left him lying in the slush.

We need a place for older citizens to play, instead of sitting in a chair eating gruel all day; someplace where we can wear our hats backwards, too, and let our pants droop down so low that the crotch is dragging on the ground.

Society has to start doing more for its pensioners before they get ugly and start rioting.

Now you take Mary Johnston. Mary is getting up there. I don't know just exactly how old Mary is, but she dated Abe Lincoln a few times before he grew that ridiculous beard. A skateboard park would be an ideal place for her to fool around while she's waiting for her phone call from the school board. Mary is a teacher. Once teachers retire, the board calls them every morning at 5 a.m. to supply for the younger members of the staff who were downsized by Dave Johnson, the Minister of Education. (Dave is the big tall geek who combs his hair over his bald spot. You're probably thinking of Ernie Eaves who combs his straight back and looks like he should be carrying a machine gun or driving a getaway car for Al Capone.)

Mary, and hundreds of older folks like her, needs a place to burn off their excess energy. On her teacher's pension, she can't just hop a plane and fly to Thunder Bay every weekend to shoot down the big ski jump they have for the Nordic types and the simple minded. Mary can't slip down to the Okefenokee Swamp to get in on the Friday afternoon alligator wrestling, water-ski in the Cypress Gardens Follies, or partake in the Olympic limbo trials in Jamaica.

We need to have a seniors' athletic centre right here in the Sunshine City. If the last council were still in power, we would have one. They understood the needs of seniors — probably because most of them had seen a few summers themselves — like about 75.

Over in Collingwood, they have a giant waterslide, 40 feet high, where kids can reach speeds of 70 miles an hour before they slam into some poor sap dog-paddling by in the pool at the bottom. We could build one just like it in Tudhope Park only higher. The only requirement to get in would be the stub from last month's pension cheque or the label from a bottle of Geritol. (Actually, I don't suppose folks buy that much Geritol today now that scotch is down to 20 bucks a bottle.)

Better still, we'll build the slide in Victoria Park, that way the ambulance will only have to drive a block and a half to the Emergency Ward door. What happens to the maimed after that is any-body's guess — they'll probably get shipped to Kenora or New Liskeard to lie in the hall until they can find them a bed.

Instead of the Legion spending all that money on Minor Ball, why not siphon off a couple of grand and set up a Fastball league for every-one over 70? I'm not talking about Slo-Pitch (Slo-Pitch is an excellent game, every girl should play it), I mean Fastball. Now that's a game. There's nothing like the feeling you get when some big, mean sucker fires a rock-hard ball at you at 90 miles an hour. That's a sport us nim-bler athletes (seasoned, I think they call us) can understand.

What about a soccer league for seniors? Lacrosse? I'll bet we can find a dozen guys from the Minto Cup team of '37 who would be glad to pull on the old supporter one last time.

There are all kinds of things that we could be doing to keep active — by "we" I'm not talking about "me". It's all I can do at my age to sit up in a chair and eat my gruel.

At the official opening of Toronto's nude beach in 1999, some guy showed up dressed as Queen Victoria. I don't think it was Queen Vickie herself. I'm pretty sure she passed away a few years ago.

Skinny-dippin' in the big city

I'm sure you all know by now that Toronto's first nude beach officially opened on May 24. And opened very well, as a matter of fact with a visit by Queen Victoria. It takes a great deal of courage to stand before royalty without any pants on (especially after you've just waded out of ice-cold water), but a number of the local nudists did it.

No doubt there was, and will continue to be, opposition from churches and family groups about the dangers of public nudity, but I suspect that just like the topless thing of two or three years ago, it will all go away. I am surprised that not one of the provincial party leaders jumped on the bandwagon and pledged their support for the bare bottom movement. For one thing, nudism is good for the economy. It may have a negative impact on the bathing suit manufacturers, but I'm sure that the Coppertone people will notice a dramatic increase in suntan lotion sales now that it's legal to tan a few places that in the past never saw the light of day.

The YMCA and the fitness clubs will also be high on the list of supporters — or should be. It's one thing to carry around a couple grams of extra weight when you can cover it up with a muumuu or a circus tent. It's quite another to parade your love handles up and down the beach under the scrutiny of your fellow nudists and other well-wishers from the community.

The Bug-Off makers will have to run double shifts to keep up with the demand for sprays and lotions to keep bugs, hornets, wasps, honey bees, and of course, the pesky African tsetse fly away from your secret parts.

An old friend of mine, Ron Payne, is the guy who did the DEEP WOODS commercial. He should be called back by the ad agency to make a few more. This time it will be cheaper. He won't have to buy a plaid shirt.

A nude beach in Toronto will be wonderful news for the Spalding Company, who makes volleyballs. If I remember the pictures from the nudist magazines I hid under my mattress as a kid, nudists play a lot of volleyball. Come to think of it, I wonder if teenage nudist boys hide pictures of ladies fully clothed under their beds?

The one person who is never out of work is the volleyball instructor at the TanBottom Nature Camp. Which reminds me, bee stings are not the major cause of injury at a nude beach. The greatest single drain on the Ontario Health Plan in the summer is not insect bites, but third degree burns caused when a tired volleyball player drops his sagging bottom on a red hot metal chair. Ask any health professional, the most frequent sight in hospitals in June and July is a fiery red bottom being wheeled through the corridors on its way to the Burn Unit.

I don't want to get into partisan politics so close to an election (none of them will pay me off), but if I was Mike I would be pumping a few more millions into Elizabeth Witmer's health budget to buy a few more screens. It's one thing to visit a hospital at night and see someone lying in a corridor in a cast. It's quite another to see someone's bottom glowing in the dark.

Now I am certainly not in favour of turning Couchiching Park into a nature camp. Nor do I expect Wasaga Beach to advertise the "World's Longest Freshwater Nudist Beach," but surely it wouldn't hurt either place to rope off a section where the bathers could parade *au natural* until the winter winds come down from the north and take the pleasure out of it.

I would think the best place at Wasaga would be out in front of the Dard where the New VR has its telecam. If you think Rollicking Roger giggles a lot now, wait till he's zeroing in on a bevy of unclad beauties — he'll be positively insane.

Of course, nude sunbathing is not all that it's cracked to be (no pun intended). There is a downside to lying on a beach sans garments. For one thing, there is the ever-present danger of sand fleas, and of course, the sand itself. After an hour or so of romping in the dunes, it usually takes a half hour under a high-pressure fire hose before it's safe to put on your drawers. If you think it's uncomfortable sitting around in a wet sandy bathing suit, wait till you try sitting around without it. Some of the wealthier resorts on the Riviera have beach attendants who do nothing all day but wander around with a whisk — or for the people like myself who have put on a few extra pounds over the years, a push broom.

I'll probably see all of you this summer on Toronto's nude beach — and when I say all, I mean all.

I'd like a Speedo bathing suit, please. Do they come in extra-large?

Carbohydrate overloading

I read an excellent article in the weekend *National Post* about Ironman competitors. I've started to read the *Post* now and then. It's my way of contributing money back to the hand that feeds me, although not very much. I suspect that the few shekels I draw out of the corporation every week are not sending Conrad and Barbara Black to the food bank.

I used to think that working for a newspaper was where the big money was, until the day I saw Mark Bisset from the *Packet* and Tom Villemaire from the *Enterprise-Bulletin* fighting a flock of gulls for a left-over hamburger bun.

The Ironman article that impressed me so much was about a couple of newlyweds, Lori Bowden and Peter Reid, who both placed first in the Australian Ironman Triathlon.

The couple apparently have kept their names. That seems to be happening a lot now for some reason. I can think of several high-profile married couples who decided to continue on down the road of life as if they just met in a bar somewhere. Some do it for professional reasons, while others try to keep it quiet, like Maureen Mateer. Well if you were married to Joe Clark wouldn't you?

To be honest, I didn't pick up the article because it was about athletes. What caught my eye was a big colour picture of Lori in a spandex suit, or whatever that material is that appears to be sprayed or dabbed on with a sponge. I'm not sure whether it was my keen interest in fashion that kept my eyeballs riveted on the page or the fact that I could count her ribs.

I like to watch Ironman competitions on TV. It's part of my continuing quest to reach physical perfection. I noticed, however, that Lori and Peter seem to be using a different training programme than the one I have chosen to reach my goal.

For one thing they don't eat. Oh, every week or so they nibble on some high protein snack made from kelp or any one of a dozen weeds found on the bottom of stagnant ponds. I, on the other hand, am heavily ("heavily" being the operative word here) into carbohydrate loading, which means packing in a bathtub full of pasta the day before a race.

For most people this works. However since I am impatient, I carry it to the extreme. I load up for six weeks before the big race and then top it off by missing the race altogether. For some reason, Lori looks much better in a spandex than I do in my outfit. I suspect that it's because she can afford to buy a designer spandex, while I have to wear a jogging suit that I picked up at a clearance sale at Barrie Tent and Awning.

Except for that small difference in our training programmes, their daily routine and mine are pretty much the same. They get up a 5 a.m. to run. I get up at 5 a.m. with the runs. They swim for 90 minutes. I stand in the shower for 90 minutes, or until the man from the City Works department sticks his head through the bathroom door and shouts, "Does the phrase 'water conservation' mean anything to you at all?" They take a two-hour bike ride. I drive down to the coffee shop. They run for 40 minutes. I have an apple fritter. They lift weights. I try to pick up my shoes. As you can see, it's much the same.

I could have been an Ironman athlete, but I have some problems with the events. To start, there's a 2.4-mile swim. Swimming was never my strong point. I suspect that it all started back at Danforth Tech in Toronto where I took swimming lessons when I was 8. We had to swim barenaked. I could never quite master the knack of covering myself with both hands and flutter kicking at the same time. I seem to remember spending a lot of time on the bottom of the pool with my nose rubbing along the tiles. Plus, I never learned to open my eyes under water, which is quite a drawback when you are swimming in a pool of naked persons. I'm afraid I developed quite a reputation. To this day, my picture is on the wall by their pool with a big red circle around it and an "X" across my face.

Bicycle riding is another problem. A 112-mile race may be easy for most athletes, but not for a man whose feet slipped off the pedals when he was ten, so he landed on the cross bar. I sang soprano in the church choir until I was 44.

Of course, the 26-mile run is a snap. That I can do — although they seem to do it in a couple of hours, while I require a couple of weeks. I suppose if I was to buy a pair of marathon running shoes I could do it, but it hardly seems worth paying 150 bucks for a pair of runners just to shave two weeks off my running time.

Maybe I should start working at it a bit harder. The world championships are in Hawaii in October. I might enter. First, I'll call my personal trainer, Marlon Brando, to have him work out my training schedule. I like Marlon. Standing beside him, even I look good.

Now where can I buy a one-size-fits-all spandex body suit?

I seem to have put on a few tons over the winter.

Skinny Svend doesn't represent me

Am I the only columnist in Canada with the courage to say the truth about how Canada feels about Svend Robinson? He should be asked to leave Parliament. Not because he is against having the word "God" in the Canadian Charter, but because he is skinny. How can a man represent the people of Canada if he has never known the agony of stepping on a set of penny scales and have the machine spit out a fortune that says, "One at a time please."

How can he hope to understand the trials of us "people of girth" if he has never suffered the embarrassment of being measured for a pair of pants and having the salesperson call across a busy store, "More tape."

A beanpole like Svend can't expect to understand the grief of a man being asked to wait until the roller coaster gets to the top before stepping on to avoid over-heating the motors. He has never known the humiliation of lying on the seashore while hundreds of meddling do-gooders scream, "Whale on the beach! Whale on the beach!" and try to roll you into the water.

What does Svend Robinson know of the heartache that the average Canadian feels when little children point at them and hide behind their mothers? He should be asked to step down and give his seat to the runner-up in his riding — providing of course, the runner-up isn't a skinny wretch like him.

Life is not easy for people like me. You can imagine how I must feel having to take my pants to a tailor every other month to have the waist-line let out two or three inches. I've even started rotating tailors hoping that he or she won't remember that I was just in a month before. I've started making up elaborate stories to cover my embarrassment. "Look at this nice pair of pants that Marlon Brando sent me. Do you think you might be able to find some material that matches so you can sew a whole new bum section into the back? If it isn't quite the same colour, don't worry. I've started to wear a one-size-fits-all beer shirt over everything and it hangs right down past my ankles."

I'm still wearing the same pair of jeans I wore when I went to high school, but I can only pull them up to my knees and I have to borrow Michael Jordan's suspenders to keep them up. Even then, I can't do up the fly.

I have such a problem keeping my dress pants up over my pot, I've started to use tacks. It hurts a bit but at least the crotch of my pants doesn't drag on the ground.

I can no longer shop at a men's wear store. I go over to the local Co-Op after dark. One of the kinder clerks slips a pair of Junior Sample's overalls out the window. If you don't remember who Junior Sample is, he's the big fat guy on *Hee Haw,* who was so big that they used to show full-length movies on the back of his boxer shorts when the drive-in closed for the winter.

I am too wide to fit in an airplane seat. The last time my dad and I flew to Winnipeg, he sat in first class, and I was strapped to a luggage rack somewhere in the tail, and damn near froze to death.

At least I wasn't lonely — Roseanne was back there with me. They brought our lunch just as we were flying over the Sault — a whole ox. By the time we passed over Thunder Bay, we were down to the hooves and had to ask the cargo attendant to bring us a firkin of ale to wash it all down.

I've tried all the diets, but they never seem to work. Perhaps if I didn't try them all at one meal it might make a difference. I bought a half dozen of the Lite Delight products. They were delicious, but a six-pack was hardly enough. I had to supplement them with a Slim Fast milkshake with a big scoop of Laura Secord ice cream floating on top. (I rushed out and bought the entire inventory before the

Americans who bought the company watered the stuff down like they do with their beer.)

No, my friends, Svend Robinson does not represent me and he certainly doesn't represent the rest of you. I've seen you waddling down Main Street. Most of you are just like me. Don't forget, I was beside you when the bus driver asked you to sit on one side all by yourself so his bus wouldn't roll over going around a curve. I remember the time the escalator ground to a halt in the Eaton's Centre trapping you between floors and they had to lift you off with a crane. I saw the look on your face when you climbed in the truck at the Automotive Show and all four tires blew off. Svend doesn't represent you either.

We need someone to be our spokesman in Parliament that knows all the everyday problems we porkers face. The only person I can think of who is built like us is Teddy Kennedy, but he's an American. There must be a tubby Canadian out there who can be our Member of Parliament. One thing for sure — it ain't Svend Robinson.

I was mad at my doctor the other day. I had been browsing through a 1952 National Geographic in his waiting room and realized he had cut out all the pictures of the ladies without their undershirts.

An easy guide to doctors' salaries

I heard the other day that Ontario is looking for more rural doctors. I might be interested in something like that as long as I don't have to actually touch the leeches. Just as a hobby, not for the money. I can't begin to spend all the money that I make for this column now. Although I suppose we could always use a few extra bucks around the house for incidental stuff — like food.

I don't know all that much about doctoring, but there must be some sort of apprenticeship program to become a member of the world's oldest profession. (Now that I think about it, the oldest might be another profession. It makes more money, but you have to work a lot of nights, and if you don't get a good corner it can get fairly lonely — especially in Moose Jaw on a Saturday night in January.)

It is not generally known outside of their of close-knit little medical organization, but doctors are paid, not by the degree of skill required to do whatever it is they do, but by the complexity of their medical designation.

For instance, a doctor who has become an expert in the treatment of say "kidneys" will be paid $72.50 per week, plus some sort of bonus system based on volume and success rate — if any. This is understandable, "kidney" being a short two-syllable word. Similarly, a "bone" doctor gets $67.50. Do you see how it works?

But doctors have found a way around these poor wages. Take a "heart" man or woman. (You can go to a "heart" woman if you want. Personally, I'm not sure that I want to take the chance of letting some lady at me with a scalpel who is hurrying to catch *All My Children* at one o'clock.) "Heart" has five letters, one syllable. This would equate to $67.50 per week. To get around that, the "heart" doctor now refers to him/herself as a cardio-vascular surgeon. Instead of working on your old pumper, he/she is now fiddling with your cardio-vasculars. Your $67.50 doctor has just hyphenated himself up to $102.50 a week. A fair chunk of change I would say.

Now look, I'm not trying to be critical of the earnings of the medical community, but it does seem a little ridiculous that a mere doctor, just by using big words and throwing in the odd colon ... oops! scratch that ... the odd hyphen, can make as much as a cleaner in housekeeping.

This, of course, has led to some serious abuses of the salary system, and is the very reason why Mike Harris and whichever bozo is Minister of Health this week are sticking their noses into the Ontario Health Services programme.

A lesser person than myself would try to pad the column at this point with some cheap medical humour. I will not. Only a person of low class would take the opportunity like this to tell you about the proctologist who came back to his hometown to look up his old friends.

The really big money, of course, is in nursing. An interesting job, it differs slightly from the world's oldest profession in the fact that while both work around men in bed, the nurse is rarely required to climb into it.

I don't know if you've ever spent much time in a hospital, but it's not much fun — especially the bedpan business. For one thing, they dress you up in a nightie that allows all your secret parts to show. And what doesn't show I suspect is video taped by that big monitor behind the bed, and broadcast on the cable network. But the worst part of a hospital visit is the tests.

I'm sure that several of you have had the joy of a barium x-ray. I had to have one. My health care professional ($92.50) thought I had an ulcer. (Later, the x-rays showed that I had somehow swallowed a whole shot glass.) The agony of barium, however, does not come from choking down a concoction reminiscent of the taste of a classroom floor after a Grade 9 chalk fight. But rather it comes from the totally degrading experience of parading through a waiting room clad only in the aforementioned Pierre Cardin nightie, backless, bottomless, and above all, tasteless. I had to rest my arms on top of a screen, sort of like Red Skelton doing his Gertrude and Heathcliffe seagull routine. My chin rested in what appeared to be an inverted plastic bra cup. Then I waited. (I suspect while the technicians set up more chairs for the invited guests who were there for the afternoon performance.)

While I was standing there, it became painfully obvious that my nightshirt just barely reached the bottom of my bottom. Once the guests were settled and the refreshments served, they raised the screen. Up went my arms and unfortunately, my nightie. While I was standing there, my x-ray guy ($77.50) became a registered medical radiation technologist, and suddenly was making $132.50 a week. I was socially ruined and he got a raise.

You might be surprised to learn that the telephone hasn't been around forever. If it had, Moses wouldn't have had to climb that mountain. God could have left the Ten Commandments on his answering machine.

What's that ringing sound?

I read an article in a millennium issue of the *Packet* that had been taken from an 1892 newspaper. It was a guide on how to use the telephone. It seems laughable today when many of us are able to dial and answer a phone with only a few weeks instruction at Georgian College, but can you imagine what a wonder a telephone must have been in the 1800s?

We take you now to the modest home of Seymour and Rachael Beitz. Their best friends, Myrtle and Archibald Goom, are visiting from far-off Barrie.

Seymour and Archibald are out in the back shed looking at Seymour's new saw. It is the most wondrous thing. By merely drawing it back and forth over a stick of wood, the little teethy things chew the stick right in half. Before that the only way to break a piece of wood in half was to put a huge boulder on one end and drop a fat person on the other.

"Well, Myrtle, the boys will be out back for a while. Seymour has a new toy."

"What a man your husband is. Every time we come here he has something new. What was it last month, a cream separator?"

"That's right, and we don't even have a cow. But he had to have one. And the month before that, it was indoor plumbing. 'We have to be the first in the village to actually have a privy inside, Rachael.' And I said, 'That's fine for you, dear, but I'm the one that has to carry the pail outside.'"

"Well, that's a man for you. Last week, Archibald brought home a thing he called a straight pen — with a steel nib, mind you. 'It will be good for the kids to do their sums at home.' Well, I just said, 'As long as the goose still has her tail feathers, there'll be no pens in this house.'"

"Aren't men something? You know what Seymour wants now? An icebox. 'The kids shouldn't have to drink sour milk, Rachael. We could buy an icebox. The man will come around every day with a block of ice to keep things cool.' Hah! It's to keep his beer cool. That's what it's for. If warm beer was good enough for my father, rest his soul, it's good enough for Seymour."

"Rachael, what's that noise?"

"What's what noise?"

"That ringing noise."

"Darned if I know. I've never heard it before. Oh dear, I hope it isn't the cream separator. I don't know why he had to put it in the parlour in the first place."

"There it goes again. Rachael, I'm frightened."

"My stars, I know what it is. It's the listening device."

"The what?"

"That black thing on the sideboard. Seymour bought it five years ago. It's the first time it has ever made a noise."

"What are you supposed to do with it?"

"I have no idea, Myrtle. I've forgotten why he bought it. It certainly is loud isn't it? Maybe I should call Seymour. I'm no good with these new-fangled things. There it goes again. Why won't it stop? Call Seymour."

"SEYMOUR!"

"Not in here, you idiot, out the back door. If there was only something we could use to call him without running outside."

"Like what?"

"I don't know — like a telephone."

"A what?"

"Oh Myrtle, how silly of me. That's what the thing is. It's a telephone."

"Why is it ringing?"

"I think someone is calling."

"I don't hear anyone."

"No, they're calling on the telephone."

"Maybe you should lie down. You look a little tired."

"No, I'm fine. I can't remember what I'm supposed to do with it."

"What if you whacked it with a stick?"

"No, it has something to do with that thing with the wire hanging on the side."

"Well, hit the thing with a stick."

"I think I'm supposed to hold it up to my ear and listen."

"We have a seashell that we do that with."

"I think if I listen I'll hear voices."

"I don't think so — only the ocean."

"I'm going to try it. Here goes — Hello."

"Mrs. Beitz?"

"Yes."

"Mrs. Beitz, I'm Percy from Murphy's Duct Cleaning Service. We just happen to be in your neighbourhood. I'm down the street cleaning your neighbour's flue. Could I drop by now, or would tomorrow morning be more convenient?"

I must have been on a technology kick the summer of '99.

Hillbillies embrace the new technology

Well, we finally did it. The Fosters moved into the 20th century.

Our friends have been after us for years to take advantage of the new technology. Even the folks at the paper have been saying for weeks, "I don't know how you two can get along without using the technology available. Spend the money and buy a new system." And reporters aren't the brightest people around. I figured if they can use the Net, then surely we can.

After all, my wife has her Grade 4 and I'm almost there. I'm taking a correspondence course, but when you can't read it takes a little longer. But it's all right for the reporters to go ahead and buy all this new-fangled equipment — they make big money. They also don't have the expenses that we have to worry about. They don't have a cat. This week we are almost out of kitty litter and that stuff is 10 bucks a bag. You ought to see what Duchess does in it — well maybe not. But everything costs so much these days. Beer and milk prices are at an all-time high and we've had to cut down. Well, not me exactly, but Sharon had to learn to drink her coffee black.

But we held a family meeting and decided to take the plunge and join the rest of the "teckies."

So many people have said that they don't know how I can write if I don't know what is going on in the world. (I said the same thing to Mike Harris.) So last Saturday, we set out early in the morning and did it. We bought a radio. We were going to go uptown and buy a new one, but there was an excellent model down the street at a garage sale — a Philco floor model with knobs on it and everything. It has a wire aerial sticking out the back that I think we were suppose to attach to a radiator. But we don't have a radiator, so we tied it to the doorknob. It works very well except every time someone opens the door, the radio falls over. So far we've been able to get stations from as far away as Barrie.

Of course, it has caused a few problems around the house. The missus is hardly speaking to me and even if she does, she's always mumbling about "damn technology."

I start "surfing" on it as soon as I wake up, and before you know it, it's midnight and I haven't got any writing done. We can't see the house next door for grass because I won't stop surfing long enough to cut it. It's so addictive. I know Sharon wants to try it, but I'm not sure that women are advanced enough technically to handle the newer stuff. She really doesn't have the patience for it. Yesterday she stood behind me all afternoon waiting to try it. Quite frankly, she was beginning to get on my nerves. Finally I said, "OK, if it's that important, go ahead." But by then it was eleven o'clock and she had gone to bed.

Communication is so important nowadays. I don't know how we kept up before we bought the Philco. You can even talk to your neighbours on it. Well not exactly talk, but if we stick a fork in the back where all those tubes and wires are, all the neighbours will come to the door to see what the hell we are doing.

It has been a wonderful thing really. Now in the morning we turn on Jack and Heather and catch the weather report. That in itself, is worth the $5 we paid for the set. Instead of us looking out the window to see if it's raining, they look out the window and tell us what it is doing. Now when the water is pouring through the windows and under the door, we know exactly what the problem is without guessing.

If I have any regrets about spending all that money, it is the fact that technology is moving so fast that our radio will be obsolete in just a few years. Pretty soon, someone will invent something else and people will be laughing at our Philco sitting there in the living room. As a matter of fact, some of our friends are snickering now and we've only had it a week.

I only wish we had saved up a little longer and bought a newer model. Sometimes the stories and news broadcasts on the old sets are out of date. This morning I was listening to Amos and Andy and a news flash came on that our Prime Minister, Mr. Diefenbaker, had cancelled the Arrow.

Man's constant search for stupid things to do fascinates me.

Running the bulls — beef for boneheads

I'm sure you all saw the picture of the Oakville man who celebrated his graduation from Queens by running with the bulls (most people just put on a funny hat and go looking for a job).

Every year at this time, thousands of boneheads tear down the narrow streets of Pamplona, a few feet ahead of a herd of crazed bulls on their way to the arena to fight for the honour of becoming some Spaniard's dinner.

Unfortunately, our boy, Robert Stodola, was gored. He recovered, except for a hole in his arm, a nervous tic, and he can no longer walk by a meat counter without spinning around to see what's chasing him.

Why people want to run ahead of a flock of ugly animals the size of a Honda, I can't quite fathom, but I suspect the word "stupidity" must come up in the post mortem hearings quite often.

Actually, Robert got off fairly lucky with only an elbow injury. Some lunatic from Chicago can now use both facilities in a two-hole outhouse at the same time. A passing bull gave him a second outlet, which is unfortunate really since he won't be able to show his scar without risking an indecent exposure charge.

I suspect if you ask a Spaniard why anyone would want to try this brainless stunt, he would probably say that the participants do it to test their courage. I don't know many Spaniards, but I notice that they don't make it a habit of running down Highway 400 on a Sunday evening in July. I suspect Spaniards don't run at Pamplona at all. They just talk us gringos into doing it.

There is a fairly narrow line between being courageous and just being plain dumb. It's a man thing. If it is the stupidest thing you ever heard of, then some man will have to try it.

You ladies really wouldn't understand, but it is important for us chaps to impress you by doing all sorts of brainless stunts. It's much like you spending fourteen hours at the hairdresser's getting a perm, then coming home and washing it out.

The whole bull thing is a throw back to when man was a cave person and won the hand of a woman by doing a series of valiant deeds — like whacking a dinosaur with a rock.

The problem today is we men have so few places to test our courage here in Canada. We haven't had a herd of bulls run down the main street for several weeks, and I haven't seen a dinosaur since the last time I was in Ottawa and visited the Senate.

Displaying our courage is a necessary part of the courtship ritual to win the heart of a fair damsel. We do it to show her that we are willing to risk life and limb to win her hand — or whatever part we are interested in.

It is difficult to show the girl of our dreams (or our wives either) that we are brave and manly.

Fortunately, I can suggest a few things that will impress her and won't require a plane ticket to Spain or a reservation at Pamplona General.

Prove your manliness to your loved one by clever repartee. The next time your wife says, "How did you find my meat loaf?" Simply reply, "It was easy. I followed the smoke." She will be ever so surprised and will appreciate your honesty. She'll kill you, of course, but she will certainly admire your courage.

When you come home and your wife is wearing a mudpack, say "Yeah, I like that better."

Another way that I find effective is to be more assertive. Don't be wishy-washy anymore. Tonight just stand up and announce, "I'm going out." And when your missus says, "Will you take out the garbage on your way?" You say, "You cooked it. You take it out." (I stole that from an old Marx Brother's routine. It worked for Groucho. He was married thirty-six times and ended up in a mental institution — the logic escapes me.)

Just by saying these three witticisms you will have proved your courage and yet have no bull holes in you. On the other hand, you are probably lying in the Emergency Ward with cuts and abrasions, while a nurse asks you how many fingers she's holding up. But the point is, you have shown your wife how brave you are. Of course, you have also earned the right to sleep in the garage for the rest of the summer, but there is always a price to pay for being manly.

For instance, right now my wife is in the shower and I am standing beside the hot water tap. Do I have the courage or don't I?

The scariest thing about this column is most of it is true.

A country bumpkin in the big city

Last Wednesday I went to the big city. Why is it whenever we country boys go to Toronto we act like Li'l Abner on his first visit to Bugtussle, Tennessee?

I was walking along Front Street at noon hour and somebody blew a car horn. So, I waved. Only a yoyo from the north woods would be dumb enough to think someone recognized him in a city of three million people.

Try as I might, I just can't seem to blend in with the general population. I always feel like I stick out like a sore thumb, and I probably do. City people are quick to recognize a rube when one drops in for the day. It's a good thing that there wasn't a reporter from the *National Post* looking for a story. I can see the news item now.

Hick seen on Yonge Street

Well-known hayseed, Mr. James Foster, made his annual pilgrimage to Toronto today. Mr. Foster was nattily attired in a pair of designer overalls off the rack at Ferguson's Farm and Feed. His pant legs (about 3" too short) were stylishly baggy with what appeared to be mud or animal droppings smeared on the knees. His grey work socks, with the red band around the top (Co-Op, 1949 — two pairs for $1.98), showed briefly above his black boots (unlaced with the tongues flapping), barely covering his long underwear. Mr. Foster's shirt, a nondescript yellow plaid of a flannel-like material, was accented by a red tartan tie — probably a clip-on. Completing his ensemble was a hat of some sort of straw to match the one sticking out of his mouth.

It was obvious to this reporter that the clodhopper was in the city trying to peddle a book, since a number of crayon scribbled papers were sticking out the top of his IGA bag. Had the yokel contacted the Toronto Board of Trade beforehand, a ticker tape parade could have been arranged to welcome him to civilization.

Reports that the same gentleman was seen ogling the secretaries leaving the Royal Bank building and shouting, "23 Skidoo," have not been confirmed. Although, police records show that a man matching his description was seen walking up Bay Street carrying a naked mannequin.

I am not comfortable in the city. Whenever I'm on the subway, I have the strange feeling that the locals are staring at me — and the locals themselves look like they are out of a day pass from the Metropolitan Zoo.

There was a lawyer across from me wearing a dark grey business suit and white running shoes. I knew he was a lawyer because he had beady eyes and was carrying a brief case big enough to hold twenty-four beers and the engine from a '64 Buick Roadmaster.

Of course, there was the usual guy sleeping. People who sleep on the subway fascinate me. I'm always afraid that some hood will roll them while they are off in Dreamland. Meanwhile, I'm sitting there with my back to the corner, one hand over my wallet, and my money sewn into my underwear, with both feet pointed to the door in case I have to make a break for it.

Plus, I worry that he will miss his stop.

It's true. One afternoon I had to stand, and there was a guy sleeping. He never once opened his eyes. When we reached Eglinton West, his eyes popped open and he got off the car. He probably went home and told his wife that some bozo was staring at him all the way from Union Station.

This time there was a girl a few seats up with one of those skirts with buttons right to the floor, but open all the way up to next Tuesday. I didn't know whether she knew that her bare leg was hanging out or if I should tell her. I hate that. A gentleman doesn't stare at a woman's bare leg. But where do you stare? You can't read a Preparation H sign all the way to Yorkdale. It's the same with a low-cut blouse. Where do you look? I once saw a girl with immense cleavage in the Eaton's Centre. I was gawking and fell down an escalator. The escalator was going up. If you fall down a flight of stairs you will eventually reach the bottom. Escalators go on forever. (I didn't make that up. That's a line of Lorne Elliot. I heard it on the CBC. I'm not stealing it — just borrowing it for a while.)

"AOORYUAEGHRTTOUR"

Excuse me, that's the subway P.A. system telling me it's my stop. Either that or the driver is telling that girl that all her buttons are undone and her bare leg is hanging out.

I pride myself in the ability to say the dumbest thing at the worst possible time. There is nothing that will make an old classmate happier than to know that he or she is reasonably intelligent, and you are still in the knuckle-dragging stage.

Thank heavens your face cleared up

There's another reunion coming up on Labour Day weekend.

Don't you just love reunions? It's a chance to get together with old friends, an opportunity to re-live old memories, and finally a chance to find out why little Mary Wedgewood had to stay with her aunt three years in a row.

Sometimes the best way to enjoy these little get-togethers is to wander through the crowd and listen to snippets of conversations. You hear the strangest things:

"Don't tell me that you are Skinny Minnie Melrose. Why you were no bigger than a minute. Well you certainly look lovely. You've filled out. I love your slacks. It's amazing how far that material will stretch. Come on into the next room, there's some people you will want to meet. Ralph! Larry! Come over here and give me a hand to shove Minnie through the doorway. Oh, and grab that bottle of Mazola oil, we might need it."

"Fred, I see you still have a tooth."

"I can't get over it. You haven't a grey hair on your head and you're 64 years old. Was your hair always the colour of oxblood shoes? By the way, you might want to slip into the washroom with a pot of glue. Every time the fan swings our way, your hairpiece hovers like a helicopter landing at the O.P.P. building."

"Oh, Mervin, you always were a snappy dresser. Now where did you buy a pale blue leisure suit in 1999?"

"So this is your boy Rufus. I never would have guessed. It sounds silly, but he is the spitting image of young Bernie Winkle who lived next door to your wife just before the two of you got married. On the other hand, it may just be the way the light is shining on his big nose."

"Now they tell me, Bert, you were a guard at Kingston for twenty years... . Oh, you were under guard at Kingston for twenty years .... No kidding ... with an axe? Well quite frankly, I don't know how you put up with her in the first place."

"Have you met my wife, Jane? Oh I forgot the two of you were married for a few years. Are you still having the same problem? Thank God for Viagra, eh?"

"I was sorry to hear about your divorce. Your own brother, I understand. Well, I guess it wasn't the first time. You remember that time she was in the shower with the basketball team and ... oh, you didn't know about that. Well, it's all water down the old shower room drain, I suppose. Are you OK? You look a little pale. Here I'll get you a drink. You can't? A.A. Well, I'm sure one won't hurt you. Oh, bartender, a couple of double scotches over here."

Reunions are great fun, but there are a few words of wisdom I should lay on you before you show up at the Legion and make a total ass of yourself.

If your husband neglects to introduce you to an old school chum, don't get insulted and go and sit in the car. It isn't because he is ashamed of you. (Although he might be. Most wives take the curlers out of their hair before they get to the reunion.) He is desperately trying to remember who this bozo is. I find the best way to handle the situation is to say, "Have you met Sharon? Sharon this is ... OH LOOK THERE'S JIMMY HILL. JIM, COME OVER HERE. Well it was nice meeting you, Mmmmph. I'll see you around.

"Jim, who is that idiot I was just talking to?"

Before you bring up the time we all went skinny-dipping, make sure that the wife your friend is standing with isn't the same girl who wouldn't get out of the water until we all turned around.

Another thing, don't say, "Thank heavens, your face cleared up. Now if you could only do something about those warts."

If you see an old teacher, don't take it upon yourself to verbally attack him because he failed you. Remember, he may remember the results of your I.Q. test. It won't do your reputation much good to have the whole room hear that your intelligence level is just above that of a garden slug, but not as high as a toad.

If you see an old girlfriend, think twice before you talk about that night at the drive-in. Some spouses, believe it or not, are not that impressed how fast the two of you fogged up a window. But if you really must, make sure you have your Ontario Health Card in your wallet.

"Composting for Fun and Profit" and other works of B.S.

Composting for dummies — a user's guide

Sunday morning I took my annual trip out to the backyard to check on the biological goings on in our composter.

Someone told me that it takes time to break all the stuff down, so I don't make it a habit of running out every hour to see if it's working. But once a year for sure, I go out and stick my head down the hole to see what's wonders have been happening over the past twelve months.

Last summer, we had a hornet's nest in there, but they moved out when the bees took over the west wing. I don't recommend sticking your head in a bee's nest. My head swelled two hat sizes in five minutes. The next morning, a man from the Beehive Honey company offered me ten dollars for my head. I was a little reluctant, but Sharon was ready to sign on the spot.

The annual trip to the composter used to be a family affair. Lately, I've noticed my wife is no longer giddy with anticipation to see how things are coming along. In the beginning, she would get all dressed up, maybe put on her string of pearl (we are saving for another) but last year she just wore an old pair of shorts with paint all over them and a one-size-fits-nobody beer shirt. This summer she didn't even bother making the trip at all.

I admit the whole thing is discouraging. The neighbours all get truckloads of fine filthy dirt from their composter, we get nothing. Well that isn't quite true. In 1994, we got a whole cupful of dirt. While I was in putting a roll of film in the camera to take a picture of it, someone stole it. This is a sick society when a person steals your dirt. I left one of my wife's casseroles out — no one swiped that. People sure have a sick sense of humour — or a strong sense of survival.

I don't know why our composter doesn't seem to work; we put stuff in it all the time. My neighbours seem to get a lot more out of theirs than we do. Every other week, a big dump truck pulls into Hughie and Marge's yard next door, fills up, leaves them a hundred bucks, and drives away. (Keep that to yourselves. I don't think they report the money on their income tax.)

I read somewhere that you were supposed to throw in vegetables. I started doing that right away. There are cans and cans of them down there, but as for compost — nothing.

This morning I took the top off to stir things up. You are supposed to flip the stuff over now and then. It's amazing what has accumulated in there over the past few years.

There's a rubber tire I found leaning against a car on the side of the highway. The driver was swearing at his jack at the time and didn't notice me. That was a year or so ago, but the tire isn't compost yet. I saw the driver again last week. He was still standing by the side of the road scratching his head. I'll give the tire another few days. If it hasn't disappeared by the weekend, I'll take it out and make a planter out of it.

I have always admired people who can decorate their front lawn with clever planters and white painted rocks. You see a lot of that in Forest Hills and the Ozarks.

I could always set the tire on fire. Although the last time I did that the police and the fire truck showed up. It's a good thing I torched it on Hughie's side of the lawn. Marge is being paroled from Beaver Creek this weekend. The family is planning a welcome home party. I guess our invitation must be lost in the mail.

There's an old shoe in there, some chicken bones, and something I can't identify, but it had a little leather collar with *Fluffy* spelled out in priceless jewels. There is a ton of stuff in there, but no compost.

I thought about phoning the city to see if I could buy a few yards of compost to throw on top. Composters may be like the old-fashioned backyard pump that you had to pour water down the top. That's another thing I never understood, why you had to pour water down a well to get it to work. What if you were lost in the desert and found a pump. You would have to walk all the way back to Cairo to get a can of water. I guess pumps are a lot like women. Quite often you have to pour a cupful of gin in them to get them started.

I'll give the composter one last try. If it still doesn't work, I'll scrap it. I'll just stick my head in and ...

Does anyone else hear a buzzing sound?

I've never been a great fan of Mike Harris. I'm sure if I was a good golfer, we would have a lot in common. But I was appalled by the media frenzy when he and his wife broke up. Nothing is sacred with some of these swine.

The right to know and other excuses for nosiness

There are times when we just have to be proud to be Canadians. It is so reassuring to know that our media still believes in the right of privacy for our prominent people; a fine example is the Mike and Janet Harris separation. It was treated as a personal decision between Mike and his missus and almost slipped by unnoticed.

Oh, it may have been mentioned every fifteen minutes for fourteen straight hours on every news channel from Tuktoyaktuk to Seal's Flipper, Newfoundland, but there was no intent to pry. It was just an honest attempt to keep the public informed in case something juicy came up that we should know about.

I was so proud of the *Toronto Star*. (I refused to look at the *Sun* in case they had Janet in nothing but her motorcycle boots on page 3)

Except for a blurb on Saturday's front page (continued on page 22), and two coloured pictures, one of Janet Harris in her shorts, and interviews with a few of their North Bay neighbours and a discussion of what this means to future on the Conservative Party nationally, the *Star* respected the Premier's request for privacy. However, if Mr. Harris really cared about the people, he would have had the decency to announce the decision earlier in the day to give the media time to round up more pictures, and perhaps get a few comments from the other provincial premiers. I'm sure that Glenn Clark would welcome the opportunity to talk about Mike — anything to take the heat off him over the B.C. casino scandal.

We take you now to North Bay, where news anchor, Lazlo Sleeze has managed to get inside the Harris family home posing as an Earwig technician.

Sleeze: Good evening, I am standing outside the bathroom door in the home of Michael and Janet Harris.

Knock! Knock!

Mrs. Harris: Who's that?

Sleeze: Mrs. Harris, it's Lazlo Sleeze of Trash News TV. May I come in?

Mrs. Harris: No you can't. I'm in the bathtub. How did you get in my house?

Sleeze: I told the kids I was here to inspect your bugs.

Mrs. Harris: We only have one bug, Sleeze, and you're it. Get out.

Sleeze: I just wanted you to know that folks from the Maritimes to Vancouver are with you all the way, and want to assure you that we will respect your right to keep your personal life out of the public eye. Now if you wouldn't mind asking a few questions, you can get back to your bath. When did you first suspect Mike of running around with that waitress?

Mrs. Harris: What? Get out of here. There are no other women involved.

Sleeze: You mean he's gay? You heard that here, folks. Janet Harris says, "Mike is a poof." Do you have any names, Mrs. Harris?

Mrs. Harris: He's not gay. Leave me alone. Wait a minute! Folks? Who are you talking to?

Sleeze: The Canadian people. We are live from coast to coast. Larry, take a shot in the laundry basket in the corner — human-interest stuff. I'll just peek in the bathroom. That's amazing. Look at all those soapsuds. What kind of bubble bath are you using? My wife's buys Mr. Bubble but it only stays around a minute and then my ducky is right there in plain view.

Mrs. Harris: Get those cameras out of here!

Sleeze: The lady next door says that she knew there was a problem back in '87 when Mike caught you voting Liberal. Is there any truth to that?

Mrs. Harris: Of course, there isn't. Besides it was NDP. I just wanted him to lose so he would get the lawn cut. He was always off campaigning somewhere. Our lawn looked like Algonquin Park. Now get out of here.

Sleeze: I'm going. I'm going. By the way there's hole in that face cloth you're holding up. Zoom in on me, Larry. This is Lazlo Sleeze, live from the bathroom of the Harris residence in North Bay. Later we will have an in-depth discussion by a team of eminent psychiatrists who will explore the causes of the separation to determine if it was masterminded by Darwin McGillicuddy, the Liberal leader, or whether it all stems from Mike's toilet training difficulties. But first, we take you now to our remote in Queens Park, where Trash News team's own Sylvia Simpson has managed to catch the Premier sitting on the john. Over to you, Syl.

Only in Orillia! All most cities have to worry about is the occasional pigeon pooping on a statue in the park. We've got big problems!

Please stoop and scoop the elephant poop

Usually it's quite a feather in the old cap to have your city featured in the big Toronto papers. But typical of Orillia's luck, we weren't centred out for some contribution to the world of the Arts, or for being on the cutting edge of a new technology. We made it because some visiting circus elephants pooped in our lake.

On the other hand, I suppose it fits right into Stevie Leacock's vision of Orillia. Something dumb like that could only happen in the mythical town of Mariposa, never in the real world.

I think we should look at this and promote this stuff — maybe even import a few more elephants from Peru or wherever they come from. Our council may not have had the vision to build a cultural centre at the Leacock home, but they will be sharp enough not to miss this opportunity. The future of our city may lie in elephant poop. Of course, they'll hold a dozen meetings, read the usual staff reports, and sometime in the fall of 2001 make a decision on what to do with this first batch. By that time, the poop will have floated to Barrie, and they will have built houses out of it or something. Knowing Janice

Laking, the mayor down there, she might even pile it beside that giant steel chicken in Kempenfelt Park as a tourist attraction. Barrie will make a fortune.

But just in case our council decides to jump into elephant poop with all sixteen feet and start our own flock to go into mass production, it wouldn't hurt for us to learn something about elephants.

For you people who had the misfortune to have been educated at schools other than ODCVI, elephants are those big grey animals with a tail at both ends. They are quite large, and some have weighed as much as the late Orson Wells, or the guy who played Frank Cannon on TV, although not all that many.

The first thing we need to look into is this fallacy that elephants are highly intelligent. Although they aren't dumb either, hey would never elect a council to be in power for three years.

You've all heard that elephants never forget. Well obviously that isn't true. Here's three that forgot to bring along a roll of toilet paper, which I assume would have to be about the size of the village of Uptergrove.

If you really stop to think about it, just what does an elephant have to remember anyway? They hardly need to worry about forgetting another one's name. They only have two or three. Have you ever seen an elephant's phone book? Dumbo, Jumbo (I forget the third one. Dolores, I think). They can't get lost. They always hang on to the tail of the guy in front. Of course, if the leader is a male, he might get lost and would be too stupid to stop and ask somebody for directions, but at least they'd all be lost together.

I suppose there is always the chance that the leader will latch on to the tail of the last elephant in the line and the whole gaggle will shuffle around in a circle until they starve to death. But them's the breaks.

I believe I read somewhere that elephants mate for life. If that is true, it probably has little to do with love and faithfulness. After all, if the missus is holding on to your tail all day, how much trouble are you really going to get into? Besides elephants all look alike, you might as well stay home. You sure couldn't keep the affair a secret for very long — all that trumpeting and trees falling down.

Most are very good at learning tricks. I suppose that requires a certain amount of intelligence, although I heard that it takes them years to learn one simple little thing — like putting their front feet up on the guy ahead of them and walking around in a circle. You know, there might just be an opening for someone with that kind of training in Mike's new cabinet.

Before we go ahead and start our own flock, I guess we better phone Bill Keller, Orillia's horticultural expert, to see if elephant droppings are good for anything.

In the meantime, if you should happen to be wading in Couchiching Park and a lump the size of a watermelon floats by, whatever you do, don't take it to the council chambers on Andrew Street. There's enough of that stuff up there already.

Why didn't this happen when Ann Boleyn was looking for one?

How to get ahead

You won't believe this, but an American has come up with something sensible. A leading brain surgeon from Case Western Reserve University has unveiled plans to perform the world's first head transplant.

What a wonderful thing this will be for you ladies. Finally you can do something about those bad hair days. No more will you have to sit there moaning to Mr. Bruce, "I simply can't do a thing with this hair." No more will you complain of split ends and frizzes. Throw all your conditioners, imported shampoos, hair sprays, gels, and styling mousses in the garbage. Pick up your phone today and dial 1-800-NEW BEAN and Dr. Robert White of Case Western will drop by with his sample case and switch your head.

And what a godsend for us lads too — especially you chaps who threw away your hairbrush years ago and start each day with a squirt of Pledge and a quick buff with a clean dry rag. Think of what a surprise it will be for your missus. She waves goodbye to Elmer Fudd and who comes home for dinner? Tom Cruise. Although you might want to check with Tom before you put in your order. He may not be all that fond of the idea — unless he's been thinking of trying to switch heads with Robert Redford.

I'm not going to miss out. I've already called for my appointment. Actually, I had been thinking about a change for some time now. Not that there is anything wrong with my own head — except for the hollow sound it makes when I bump into something, and that annoying whistle whenever there is a high wind. I would like to get one with a face that isn't quite so handsome. It's been a curse for me, you know. Oh, I'm sure that most of you would kill to have a beak like mine, but to be honest, it's no fun being incredibly good-looking — ask Tom Villemaire. All my life I have been mistaken for Cary Grant. (With Tom, it was Larry from the Three Stooges.)

It was fun in the beginning. There was nothing I liked better than signing autographs and having my picture taken with my fans. There were always women chasing me, from teenage bobbysoxers (don't forget I'm old) to blue-haired dowagers. I started to wear English riding britches and saying, "Judy, Judy, Judy," all the time. It never stops. Every time *An Affair to Remember* is on TV, we have to unplug the phone. Deborah Kerr keeps calling to ask me to meet her at the top of the Empire State Building and I'm afraid of heights.

Doris Day and Sophia Loren started bothering me. Actually, it wasn't me who had the problem with Sophia. My wife got tired of kicking her out of our house. I would have suffered a little while longer.

But where will this all end? The Brits are cloning sheep and heaven knows what else. Soon it will be humans. I think it's already started. Take a good hard look at the sitcoms on TV. Don't all the stars look alike?

Without getting into the moral issues, I wonder if we should be really doing all these alterations. There are breast reductions, tummy tucks, breast augmentations, liposuction, nose jobs, collagen injections, hair transplants, and face-lifts. Mike Harris even had an extra toe sewn on his foot. (I heard Phyllis Diller has had so many face lifts that her toes have disappeared completely.)

I'm sure some of you will remember this. A few years ago, Geraldo Riviera had the fat from his buttocks injected into his forehead. I can't remember why he thought that this was necessary. I suppose he figured we all knew where his brain was anyway, he might as well move it up and out front where everyone could see it.

What scares me is 500 years from now everybody will pick and choose who they want to look like. The whole world will be the spitting image of one of two people — me or Tom Villemaire.

I have an uncle who thinks he's a chicken. We'd send him to a psychia-trist but we need the eggs. (I'll admit that joke may be a year or two old.)

6,500 bucks? That ain't chicken feed

I listened to a fascinating news report on CBC a week or so ago. The San Diego Chicken was in London, Ontario, to open a ball game. Now dressing up like a chicken may not turn your crank, but this chicken gets 6,500 bucks a game. That ain't hens' feed. Imagine, $6,500 just to dress up in a chicken suit!

I'm sure there is more to the job. He may have to stand on a fence and crow a bit at five o'clock in the morning, and he probably has to scratch for worms in the outfield or lay eggs during the seventh inning scratch or something. But it sounds like a pretty easy way to make a few extra bucks to feather your nest. (Heh, heh, did you get that? Feather your nest? Hang onto your hat, folks, the kid has a million of them!)

But the weird schemes people come up with to make money never fail to amaze me. Some guy will dress up as a chicken, another as a Blue Jay, some even dress up like councillors, and go to meetings every Monday. At least the chicken can go back to the hen house after the game, have a beer and a few seeds, and no one knows who he is. A coun-cillor isn't so lucky. Everyone knows who they are and where they roost.

If I were going to run in the next election, I would sure want to dress up as something. I don't know what. I'll have to see what kind of costumes are available in my size. You just don't go into Tom's Men's Wear and say, "I'd like to see something in a woodpecker suit, a 42 short." I wouldn't mind dressing up for a few hours for $6,500 to be a sports mascot. What animal would depend on where you live, of course.

In Orillia, you'd have to find a terrier costume; in Barrie, a horse suit. Now that would be a little more difficult. You would need a partner for the back end of your costume. Once you get into four-legged animals, you can't make as much money. You have to split your $6,500 with the guy in the rear.

It would be a fascinating career, but it could be risky. What if you were a horse for the Barrie Colts and you fell on the ice and broke your leg? The local vet would probably have to put you down. It would be a great story for the missus to tell the grandkids though, wouldn't it? "How did gramps die, Granny?"

"Well Caspar, he fell down the steps at the Molson Centre and they had to shoot him at centre ice. The sad part was, he would have lived. The guy in the back end was the one with the broken leg."

I guess there is danger in any professional sport job. A hockey player can get injured and ruin his career. It's much the same being a mascot. The guy who plays the Toronto Blue Jay could have a heart attack leading the crowd in their seventh inning exercises and he would be finished. That would be sad. They don't bury blue jays. He'd just have to flutter into a hedge and a cat would eat him.

I keep saying "him" but I suppose being a sports animal is an equal opportunity position. There is no reason why a woman couldn't dress up like a chicken and scratch around third base. It would be a little more difficult though. She would have to go to a pet shop once a month to have her feathers plucked and her claws manicured.

Washrooms would be a problem. A man can just hop up to a public facility and stand there, but a woman would have to squeeze into a stall. And there's the problem of putting lipstick on her beak with a dozen other ladies jostling for space in front of the mirror. But I'm sure that something could be worked out that wouldn't ruffle her feathers. (Did you get that one — ruffle her feathers?) The San Diego Chicken got fired. I don't know what he did that got him in trouble with the Padres; probably couldn't keep his beak shut, but can't you see him at the UIC?

"Here's something you might want to investigate, Mr. Capon. They need a chicken with good legs at KFC on Twoonie Tuesday. Oh, tell the missus to sublet the hen house. You won't be coming home."

There is a fine line between being a professional spy and a nosy S.O.B.

Shaken, not stirred

There was an article in the *Packet* about the CIA. They're running short of spies and are have started a campaign to beef up their ranks. Naturally, I applied. Spying has always been a hobby of mine. Ask any of our neighbours with a tree outside their bedroom window.

Once I start, I don't know how long the Company (that's what we spies call the firm) will let me write this column. Once I get into top security matters, I'm sure the director will restrict my public appearances. As a matter of fact he's have already spoken to me about what I show in public — and so have the O.P.P.

I imagine I'll be away a lot spying — Tangiers, Russia, Craighurst, all those other hotspots of international intrigue. Writing a column and getting it back to Orillia in time for the editors to ruin it could be a problem. I could fax it on my shoe phone, I suppose, or send it by homing pigeon. But you know how unreliable pigeons are during hunting season, and trying to fax a 700-word message on a shoe phone is almost impossible when you have a dainty foot like mine.

This column may be a bit premature since I haven't been hired yet. I'm sure that they don't hire just any yoyo off the street. They'll probably have to check me out. We spies handle some pretty sensitive material, so the CIA will want to run a security check on me. But that will be just a formality. I shook hands with Mila Mulroney at the mall once and there was no problem. Although, now that I think about it, three Mounties held me down and frisked me. I thought Mila looked a little disappointed that she couldn't do the actual frisking. I'm not surprised. I would think that running her hands all over me is every woman's dream.

Espionage would be ideal career for a man like me. I have all the qualifications. I'm nosy and beautiful women are always winking at me. For years I've been addicted to James Bond movies. They've become an obsession. I began to suspect people were spying on me. I would never get into bed without looking under it. One night I peeked under and looked right into the eyes of our cat. It scared me so bad I wet my pants and still see a psychiatrist. The cat was cured — although she still wets her pants.

Like every red-blooded Canadian lad, I can picture myself as James Bond. I even had an ejection seat installed in my car. Well I guess mine isn't quite like your standard ejection seat like Jim has in his '59 Aston Villa. The floorboards in my car are so weak that if an enemy agent jumped into the passenger seat, he would end up on the road and be fumed to death by my faulty muffler.

I began to dress the part. I bought a tuxedo for $5.00 at a garage sale. I drink my martinis shaken not stirred. I started wearing a derby hat and carry a brolly everywhere, even when it isn't raining. I've developed a cultured British accent, and wander the streets saying, "'allo 'allo 'allo" all the time.

There are parts of the job I don't think I'll care for — like killing people and seducing women, but I guess you get used to it. It's not like I haven't done it — the killing people part. My recipe for fried bologna wiped out half of Coldwater. I'll have to learn to play cards. James Bond is really good and every movie plays *chemin de fer* in Monte Carlo. I don't even know what *chemin de fer* is; I failed French, but I think it means your horse is on fire. A spy needs to know stuff like that. A couple of times I sat in on a euchre game at the Legion, but after I shouted "snap" and "go fish" a few times, the other players suddenly remembered dental appointments and I was left there by myself.

So if some night you look out your bedroom window and see a guy in a derby hat carrying a brolly, don't phone the O.P.P. It's just me doing my bit for the good old CIA. By the way, there's a hole in your pink nightie.

I have been warning people for years that the metric/Celsius stuff would cause trouble some day. But no, no one listens anymore.

The metric system and other dumb ideas

I knew nothing good would come out of this metric thing. Did you read that the Mars space probe burned up because some goof forgot to convert imperial measurements to metric ones? I've been warning NASA about that for years. If the average Canadian isn't bright enough to understand the metric system, how in the world did they expect an American to figure it out? I am only 100-200 I.Q. points off genius and even I don't understand it — especially the "gram" stuff. Every time I buy cold meat, I'm never sure if a hundred grams is just enough to cover a Ritz cracker or whether I'll need a transport to get the stuff home. This combination imperial/metric system can't go on.

Therefore, in the interest of public safety and convenience, I have invested several hours, and a six-pack, in devising an all-new system of measurements to replace the others. It is simple and easy to remember.

The shortest unit of time is an *OhOh*, which is the precise number of milliseconds after the polls close before we realize we've made a mistake once again.

A *Willitneverend* is the opposite, the longest unit of time, and is the length of time from one OhOh to another — in Orillia a Willitneverend is three years. In Ottawa or Queens Park, it is whenever the government feels like it.

The shortest measurement of distance is *Odamn*, which is the distance from that itchy spot on your back to your fingernail — almost but not quite.

The longest distance on the other hand is an *Omigod* which is the distance from where you are when you discovered you really have to go to the bathroom badly and the nearest public washroom. There is a slightly shorter distance, *Aaah*, which is the nearest bush. However, an Aaah is always accompanied by an *Aha*, which is the distance from an Aaah to a police cruiser parked nearby.

So much for the technical measurements, now the practical every-day stuff.

Foster: The amount of grass a woman can cut in one day with a power mower, while her husband lies on the couch watching the World Series, times the number of times he has to get up to tell her she missed a patch.

Navy: The amount of dark rum needed to kill the pain of a lawn-mower running up and down a reclining gentleman's back.

Hwyrob: The number of dollars required to fill a gas tank on Friday, compared to the number of dollars required for the same amount of gas on Tuesday (*Ripoffregular*).

Rubyflush: The maximum amount of crimson colour registered on a customer's face when the attendant at the Beer Store seizes his credit card in front of thirty close friends and acquaintances.

Wishfullthink: The age a geezer tells the girl in the miniskirt he is, divided by his real age — the pathetic old weasel.

Rovershout: The number of times a homeowner has to yell "get down" at his dog before the four-legged idiot leaves the minister's leg alone.

Dickydee: The number of kids with an ice cream cart needed to destroy the economic stability of Orillia.

Brownstall: The number of staff reports requested by a council on anything to do with the Leacock Museum before making the wrong decision.

Kilogrouch: The number of km per hour a person can drive over the speed limit on a normal day compared to the number on a day when the police officer's wife (husband) has kicked him (her) out for reeking of someone else's perfume (aftershave).

Clamour: Actual number of decibels attained by wife (husband) during aforementioned perfume (aftershave) discussion.

Teeny: The size shoe a woman will ask for when first entering a shoe store.

Supertank: The size she will eventually buy and bring back the next day because they are too small.

Cheeky: The number of inches above the knee a girl can wear her short shorts before making an appearance before Judge Montgomery.

Miley: The length of the grin on Judge Montgomery's face when he dismisses the charges.

Twoaxehandlesandaplugofchewingtobacco: Width of hips of the next lady who will get ten years for far too many cheekies.

Monsterjug: The bra size that a teenage boy dreams his future wife will wear.

Flatliner: What she will actually require.

Gazillion: The number of letters I'll get for going too far this time.

I love "pop" psychology. I wish I had thought of it.

Live on "Meet Boola Boola"

I was sitting on my porcelain chair this morning catching up on my reading. We keep our library in the bathroom. It's the only room with a shelf strong enough to hold both books.

Last fall, Sharon bought a copy of *Don't Sweat the Small Stuff*, a pop psychology book that was #1 on the *New York Times* Bestseller List. It was there mostly because the author, Richard Carlson, was interviewed on *Oprah*. If you are a writer and can get on her show, you've got it made. If Oprah likes your book, you can put a down payment on that shack in Medonte, because you, my friend, can retire.

Since my book is coming out mid-November, I phoned the publisher, to see it he could line me up for a guest shot early in December to cash in on the Christmas rush. Apparently, Hounslow Press doesn't have a pipeline to the major American TV networks, and couldn't arrange the *Oprah Winfrey Show*, but they do have a few connections with some of the lesser-known stations.

Next week, I will be appearing live on *Meet Boola Boola* on the BBC (Borneo Broadcasting Corporation). I'm on with two other guests, a headhunter, who is bringing his entire collection, and a tribal medicine man who got all his medical knowledge by eating a proctologist. While I'm waiting for the canoe to pick me up, I'll review *Don't Sweat the Small Stuff*.

It is an interesting book that tells you how can have a great life by simply following Carlson's 100 helpful hints. Richard himself can have even a greater life if you buy the book this time instead of swiping it from the library.

To save you a bit of time, I have condensed his entire book into a few helpful suggestions that will lead you to a healthier and happier life without having to start the day with a beaker of vodka.

Don't sweat the small stuff and it's all small stuff.

What a wonderful piece of advice! If someone cuts you off in traffic or steals your wife, don't let him ruin your day. Call Mike Tyson and Mike will drop around to his house some night and show him the error of his ways, and why in the future he will only need to buy one earring.

Let go of the idea that gentle, relaxed people can't be super-achievers.

This is so true. I have this friend who is the dearest man. He plays golf all morning, drinks beer all afternoon, and lies on the couch until bedtime. I don't remember him ever working at all. Then one happy day, his uncle kicked off and left him a million dollars. Now he lies on the couch drinking beer all day, but he doesn't have to play golf. With a million bucks he can afford to hire a professional to do it for him.

Every day, tell at least one person something you like, admire, or appreciate about them.

To be honest, I'd stay away from this one. I met a couple on the street and I told the young lady what I liked most about her. Her husband beat the hell out of me.

Mind your own business.

What a wonderful piece of advice this is. The other day my neighbour and his wife were having a terrific argument about what time he got in the night before. I rushed right over and tried to explain that it wasn't his fault. He wanted to be home on time, but the woman he was with said he was too drunk to drive. If he had come home earlier, he could have sobered up over coffee with the man I saw climbing out his window. Maybe I shouldn't have added that. Now they are both mad at me and have some sort of restraining order against me.

But the best advice in Carlson's book is:

Nurture a plant to enhance your life.

Plants are so easy to love. They don't stay out all night, they don't burp in front of your mother, and they don't pee on your carpet like your dog. They just sit there and grow. I raised a little plant all summer. I watered it, fertilized it, and I even talked to it. Just when it grew ever so tall and we were becoming friends, three Mounties and an O.P.P. officer came and took my new friend away. Now a SWAT team has surrounded our house and a canister of tear gas just came through the front window. This time I'll take his advice and I won't "Sweat the Small Stuff" — although 10-15 in Kingston is hardly "Small Stuff."

I'm not sure why I wrote this column. It must have been after another sleepless night watching a scary movie with Sharon.

Spook show scares the wits out of all us kids

Thank heavens it's November. Once Halloween is over, I can relax and stop worrying.

I hate Halloween. It is the worst time of the year for me. Oh not because of the Satan worshipping; I stopped worrying about Satan when I realized he was Mike Harris. It's the movies that the networks show every year to scare the bejeebers out of all us little kids that worry me.

I can't let my wife get control of the clicker; she loves scary movies. If I had known that she was a horror freak I never would have married her. I would have found a nice, sweet, little woman who is just as chicken as I am. Although, it may well be that no one is as chicken as I am. My life is filled with terror because of my wife's obsession with spook shows.

Women are weird. I'm not allowed to turn on a football game, it's too violent, but it's all right for her to watch some guy in a hockey mask running up and down the street with a chainsaw. I'll tell you one thing, if you live on Elm Street, don't invite me over for dinner, 'cause

I ain't coming. As a matter of fact, if you live on an Elm Street, you're a whacko, and I don't even want to know you.

The love of horror movies is a cultural thing. Sharon comes from the hills of Coulson where axe murderers and zombies wander the side roads on a regular basis. The wealthiest man in Coulson is the village barber. The day after a full moon the werewolves are lined up for a shave all the way to Jarratt.

I have to be careful what I say here. One time I was speaking at a banquet and I said that the only difference between a werewolf and a girl from Coldwater was a werewolf is only covered in hair once a month. There was one in the crowd (not a werewolf, a girl from Coldwater). Now every time we go over to see a performance of the Village Players, I have to sit in the back row with a paper bag over my head.

I have always been afraid of scary moves. When I was a little kid, I went to the old Oxford Theatre on the Danforth to see *Abbott and Costello Meet Frankenstein*. Whenever Frankenstein showed up, every kid in the place ran to the washroom. There were so many of us in the can, the only place to pee was in some other guy's pocket.

I saw Disney's *Snow White* when I was seven. The wicked queen frightened me half to death. Now every time Queen Elizabeth invites us over to dinner, I have to lie and say that I have to cut the lawn just in case she and the wicked queen are related. If you don't think it's a possibility that there has been some witchcraft in the Royal Family, take another look at Charlie's ears.

There is a whole pile of *Friday the 13th* movies and Halloween films from 1 to 30 or 40. I haven't seen any of them.

The *Alien* movies scare me, too. I saw the first one and withdrew my name from the American Astronaut program. It's bad enough to be floating around space without any beer, but I'm not going anywhere where a monster is hiding in an air duct waiting to eat me.

Sharon has seen them all. I think she's a little bent. I only watch musicals because I know that they all have happy endings, and nobody will get cut in half with a chain saw or get gobbled up by a space lizard.

When we went to see *Phantom of the Opera*, I headed to the washroom whenever the Phantom showed up. The john was packed with the same guys who had been at the Oxford Theatre fifty years ago. Only this time they were wearing tuxedos.

Halloween is spooky. Even the trick or treaters scare me. We may think that all the ghouls and goblins running up and down your side-walk are little children, but do we really know that for sure?

Last year, I ran out of goodies and a little kid in a space suit knocked on my door about midnight. When I said I was out of candy, he vaporized my car. When I woke up, there was a bottle of 12-year-old scotch missing.

At least that's what I told my wife and the man from the insurance company.

Most people have no idea what scandalous amounts of money we writers make.

Wayne and I make far too much money

The other morning I heard Jack Latimer on EZ-Rock say that Wayne Newton had just signed a contract with the Stardust Hotel in Vegas to perform six nights a week, forty weeks a year, for the next ten years. His salary is going to be so astronomical for this gig he was embarrassed to tell anyone how much it was.

I know exactly how he feels. I feel the same way about the money I make writing. Once we writers hit the big time and start hauling in the real big bucks, we are almost ashamed to talk about it, too. All writers are like that. I see it every time I go into the newsroom. The reporters don't want the rest of the staff to know how well they are doing. They pretend to be broke — even to the point of gathering up empty pop bottles to buy coffee and wearing pants with the bum out.

A person shouldn't be raking in the kind of cash I do just for sitting at home jotting down a few words, when there are union autoworkers out there, with weeks of experience, barely scraping by at 30 bucks an hour.

Granted my words are so devilishly clever that literary historians will pick them out of the blue box and store them in some university library for hundreds of years. I'm sure that at the end of the next millennium, some professor of English literature at Oxford will be using my columns as shining examples of the Golden Years of Creative Writing.

As an example of the heights that 20th century authors and philosophers reached, he will be teaching his students that my journalistic endeavours of the late 1900s were at an intellectual level only dreamed of by the likes of Bill Shakespeare and Jean Paul Sartre. (You will note that I said "he." I believe that women will soon tire of the stress of the academic and business world and will go back to the kitchen to bake cookies or darn socks.)

When I first came home in 1995 and told Sharon how much the paper was willing to pay me for 700 or 800 words of deathless prose every week, she was amazed. In fact, she was more than amazed, she was dumbfounded. She began looking through the want ads and thumbing through the grocery ads for specials on canned beans and Kraft dinner.

You may be surprised to learn that except for the few of us at the top of the newspaper game, most writers do not make a great deal of money. The majority of the world's great authors and playwrights have had to take part-time jobs from time to time just to survive.

William Shakespeare worked as a male escort in London until he was arrested for soliciting a member of the Royal Family outside Buckingham Palace. If it had been Elizabeth, the wunth he approached, he might have got away with it, but unfortunately he put the moves on her Uncle Fred. Historians believe that Shakespeare's play *Much Ado About Nothing* was not written by him at all, but by a disgruntled noblewoman who hired him and tried to get a refund.

William Butler Yeats, one of Ireland's finest poets and one of the few who could read, had to deliver fish and chips to put food on the table. When the Pope cancelled the "'no meat on Friday'" rule, he was laid off and had to supplement his meagre income by making bombs for the IRA after his UIC ran out.

Even George Bernard Shaw fell upon hard times later on in his writing career. That is why he had to grow that long beard — to cover up the fact that he couldn't afford a tie.

James Michener, who wrote *Hawaii* and *Centennial*, wrote every day in his own home from 8:00 a.m. to 5:00 p.m. and always wore a white shirt and tie. What they didn't tell you was why he had to write at home. He couldn't afford pants. (If he's still alive, I may retract that last bit. If he isn't, it's the Gospel truth.)

My book is coming out this month and I guess the word is spreading through the financial community that I'm going to make a pile of money. Every day, a different bank sends me a credit card application. I keep applying, but every time I send in my application with my present income, the card seems to get lost in the mail.

They probably think I'm a deadbeat like Wayne Newton.

This is one of those horrible flashbacks of how goofy you looked as a kid.

Fighting in our underwear

Back in 1950, I was a cadet. All high school students in the '50s were required to have military training in case the Russian Army invaded Fesserton.

I was in the P.E. Squad. While all the other cadets marched in khaki uniforms carrying rifles, we paraded up and down the main street in our underwear. Apparently, the boys in the P.E. Squad were not exactly considered top of the line soldier material. If war broke out, I believe we were the guys the generals would send into battle with spears and pointed sticks to slow the enemy down while the real troops had lunch.

As I watched the local air cadets during the Remembrance Day service, I began to wonder if there were real P.E. squads during the Second World War. And if there were, did they ever do anything heroic?

By an amazing coincidence, this morning I just happened to stumble across a number of German military documents in the bottom of a case of Berliner Burgerbrau beer that I bought at the liquor store.

My knowledge of German is a bit limited. I only know enough to say, "Gestoppemfloppem" when someone sneezes, or "ein prosit" at

Oktoberfest when it's time to chugalug more beer. However, I was able to decipher the field reports of a pitched battle between the Grey and Simcoe Foresters P.E. Squad, and several hundred Panzer tanks just outside Paris in 1944. By comparing the German on one side of the can and matching it up with the English translation on the other, I believe my interpretation of the documents is reasonably accurate.

From the evidence presented here, I believe that the bravery of the Grey and Simcoe P.E. Squad was instrumental in turning the tide of the war and I'm recommending to Art Eggleton that their gym shorts and athletic supporters be laundered and displayed at the National War Museum in Ottawa.

This first bit of information is from the flight report of Luftwaffe Major and Iron Cross recipient Rudolph Streiger. "I was flying my Fokker-Wolf about 200 feet above the ground just south of Paris. Air Marshall Goring had mentioned in a briefing that he suspected a number of French peasants (or pheasants, his handwriting is abysmal) had started a nudist colony in the area. While I was hanging out the window with my camera, I passed over what I thought was a flock of blue and white seagulls. They seemed to be doing callisthenics and were gradually edging towards a division of Panzer tanks. The tanks were idling on the side of a road and appeared to be unaware of the gulls. It is quite possible that our Panzers had stopped to do a bit of laundry as what appeared to be a pair of long underwear was draped over a gun barrel. As I looked back, I realized that the seagulls' legs were far too skinny. I doubled back, and on the second pass I could see that it was a battalion of P.E. persons preparing to attack our tanks with a series of exercises. I would have turned around and bombed them, but I was late for Rommel's birthday party. Eva Braun herself had been hired to jump out of the cake."

This next report is from the Commander of the 7th Panzer Division.

"We had stopped along a country road to rinse out our smalls, when I noticed what I believed to be a flock of sheep running towards us doing handstands and summersaults. As they neared, they suddenly began throwing volleyballs. And it occurred to me that they were pretty ugly for sheep. Fortunately, we were able to distract them by saying, 'Look out behind you.' By the time they had stopped and turned around, we managed to get back into the tanks and get the hatches closed. They attacked us with volleyballs and the noise was bedlam. I was just about to open fire, when they drew back and began to change into fuchsia danskins. Rather than subject my battle-weary troops to such a disgusting sight, I raised the white flag."

Based on this evidence, I believe that the Grey and Simcoe Foresters P.E. Squad should be given a commendation and we should be given one more statutory holiday.

Did you know that Tarzan had a daughter?

What else was going on in that jungle?

The last thing I want to do is cause more trouble for Edgar Rice Burroughs. As you no doubt know, the man hasn't even been out of the house since his sister, Mandy Rice Davies, got picked up by the fuzz during the Profumo scandal back in the late '60s.

I was rowing the Net last weekend. (That's just like "surfing the net," only much slower). Out of curiosity I went looking for Tarzan. (I had just stepped out of the shower. My resemblance to the blond-haired guy who plays Tarzan on TV is uncanny.)

I never knew, till then, that Tarzan had a daughter. Her name was Tora. Where did she come from? Now look, I've tried to be fair about this. I was willing to overlook "Boy." Hollywood sort of glossed that over. I can't remember whether Jane and Johnny Weismueller found him under a stump somewhere or whether he was their son. I have to assume they found him. Tarzan, being English and therefore Anglican, it was highly unlikely that he and Jane would have slept together until after a visit by Bishop Tutu.

On the other hand, we never heard where Jane came from. For all we know she could have come from an escort service in Nairobi. But I can't accept the fact that the two of them had a daughter. What kind of life would that be for a young girl, running around wearing nothing but a handful of leaves and living in a tree with a bunch of chimpanzees?

That's no way to bring up a young lady. Oh, her brother, Boy, would have made out OK. (You can see right away that his parents weren't too bright. A thousand names in the name book and all they can come up with is "Boy" — Boy Weismueller. At least they didn't name him after Buster Crabbe, a man named for a social disease.) Of course, Boy would make out all right. Most boys are bozos anyway. As long as he could find a pair of baggy pants and a ball cap to wear backwards, he'd survive, but a young lady? Girls have to be brought up properly even in the jungle, with their own bathroom, or I suppose, log. She'll need shoes — acres and acres of shoes.

Girls have to soak in a tub with nice smelling bath salts, not wallow in a smelly jungle pond with hippopotami and crocodiles. She has to go to the hairdresser every week, and have her hair tinted and bobbed or whatever is the rage this week.

She has to go to finishing school to learn how to pour tea and burp into a hanky like a lady. A girl has to have a purse and pretty dresses, with silk ribbons for her hair, not carry a 12" dagger and wear a loincloth carved off a leopard's bum. No, I can't believe that Edgar would have allowed this sort of thing to happen. It's too dangerous in the jungle for a girl. There are man-eating plants in every planter, and giant spiders lurking behind every bush ready to gobble them up.

Girls are afraid of spiders. (So are boys. I saw one squiggle across the kitchen floor the other day and I had to hide in the closet with the cat until Sharon came home. She is afraid of them, too. The three of us stayed in the closet all afternoon until Kirsten, our papergirl, whacked it with a *Packet*.)

How is Tora supposed to learn to be a lady living in the jungle? To start with ladies are supposed to be taught to do their nails and carry on stimulating conversations about art and classical music and stuff. How is she going to learn all that from a man whose entire vocabulary can be printed on the back of a cigarette package and still have room for a calendar, a picture a Scottish girl in a kilt, and a warning about the dangers of smoking while he's pregnant.

But what is more important and really worries me is what if she meets a nice young man, maybe a missionary's son? How is he going to impress her? Her old man strangles lions with his bare hands for a living and swings from tree to tree on a vine. Here is a guy who can't watch kitty cats on the Discovery Channel without wetting his pants, and can't climb two steps up a ladder without getting a nosebleed trying to win her heart. He'll be lucky if she doesn't cut his out.

This was written a few days after a gentleman got himself caught between the toilet seat and the bowl in a Starbucks. I would go into more detail, but I get woozy just thinking about it.

It's been a bad year for Babs Streisand

I'm sure you read that Barbara Streisand's furniture was auctioned off back in November. It's a shame really; she seemed to be doing so well. Such is life, one minute you are the toast of Broadway and the next you are just toast.

I suppose there are a lot of additional expenses when you are a star that the rest of us don't have. She probably has to get her hair done every two or three weeks and that adds up. And shoes — a girl has to have a half-decent pair if she's going to be interviewed on the *Rosie O'Donnell Show*. You don't go on national TV with your sole flapping.

At least Babs made a few bucks at the sale. Her tables, lamps, and chairs brought in just under $3 million, which will put a fair dent in the cost of a pair of brogans, with a buck or two left over to keep her hubby, Jimmy, in Viagra for a year or two. An oak and wrought iron sideboard sold for $596,500. A three-tiered table that she bought at Leon's for $35, went for $244,500, and Barbara doesn't have to pay the 35 bucks until January 2001.

More stuff was going on the auction block last Thursday. Hopefully, we will hear how she made out. If the sale bombs, we won't be able to hold a tag day for her for a while. The Salvation Army has every liquor store from here to Hong Kong tied up until Christmas.

I must say I was surprised when I looked over her sale list: there was the odd item missing that I assumed Babs would have. I didn't see a padded toilet seat. Wouldn't you think the best singer in the world would have a padded toilet seat? We even have one at our house, granted we couldn't afford a new one. We bought ours pre-owned. There's a rip down one side and a big dent in the frame like someone hit it with a crowbar. The man from Starbuck's said it had been involved in some sort of accident. If you hold it up to your ear, you can hear a guy screaming and his lawyer ordering a new Ferrari.

Now that I am a famous author, it occurred to us that perhaps we could cash in on the publicity and put some of my old treasures up for auction. With a bit of luck we might even make a few bucks for Christmas. Last year all we could afford was a can of turkey flakes.

You might want to skim through the list to see if there is anything that you might want — either for yourself or to give to someone you don't like.

There is a pair of wooden lamps that I bought at a garage sale. The first owner said they had been hand-carved by someone famous, but he had forgotten his name. He was asking $495.00 apiece, but I talked him down to 5 bucks for the pair of them. I heard him say to his wife, "Guess what? The idiot bought them." I'm starting to think the carver wasn't famous at all.

There's a lazy boy chair that I can let someone have for a C-note. All it needs is some upholstery, a few springs, and some WD-40. I put it out by the road last June hoping that someone might take it. A plough ran over it in February. So, I had to drag it in and store it in the garden shed with my dining room suite. I guess it really isn't one of your better dining room suites. It's a plastic TV table with two folding chairs I borrowed from a funeral home. We don't entertain all that much.

There is a valuable painting from my art collection that I might consider selling if I can get the right price. Although, I have to admit it will pain me. I have always been a sucker for great art. How the artist got the bulldog to sit there with four aces and not crack a smile amazes me.

We have three coffee makers without the glass carafe things for sale. I break one every other week. It's cheaper to buy a new one than replace the carafe. If I didn't know better, I would think that Al Capone didn't die after all. He's the CEO of Proctor-Silex.

There are five Melmac cups and saucers that we gave to someone as a wedding present. They were returned along with a bill for two dinners. We can only sell three saucers. We had them made into earrings. They are for my mother for Christmas.

This column was written a week after the millennium, but read by very few since the world was destroyed on New Year's Eve in a cataclysmic explosion.

Cow cream touted as udderly miraculous

If you are reading this column I have to assume that the world didn't come to an end last Friday at midnight. Of course, it may well be that just you and I survived and everyone else is just so much radioactive space dust.

It was quite a problem trying to decide what to write this time since no one was really sure that we wouldn't all be freezing in our beds with no electricity, no TV, or worse, no beer. I could have waited until New Year's morning to write this epistle I suppose, and then jot down the resolutions I broke in the first eight hours of 2000, but this being Orillia, there is always going to be something goofy to write about.

I had hoped that 1999 would have ended with the news that Orillians had finally moved into the 19th century and stopped believing in miracle cures, like mayonnaise head rubs for falling hair, and applesauce enemas for the relief of haemorrhoids. But alas, I heard on Jack and Heather's EZ-Rock morning show that our citizens are now buying up cases of Bag Balm to keep their skin young and wrinkle-free.

In case you missed the show, Bag Balm is a cream that dairy persons rub on cows' udders to keep them from drying out or exploding or something. Most of us city folks know zilch about raising cattle, and the little problems that Elsie faces each day just to supply us with cream for our coffee. Very few of us even know where the udders are let alone worry whether they dry up and fall off.

Granted some of us have rural beginnings and like to keep a hand in. Some still keep salt blocks beside the table for the occasional lick when the wife's lasagna tastes a little flat. But for the most part, we are blissfully unaware of the perils of the dairy industry, and rarely are we seen lined up at the Co-Op for the Annual Boxing Day Udder Cream Sale.

This year it's different however. The word got out that Shania Twain rubs the stuff on her skin to keep it soft and beautiful — especially around her belly button, which seems to be showing most of the time.

The strangest thing about this latest miracle cream is the stuff actually works. Eileen McGarvey and I have been rubbing it on Pete for several weeks now and he's beginning to look like a Twain. Unfortunately, he's now the spitting image of Mark, not Shania. Nevertheless, we'll keep on rubbing — anything will be better than what we started out with.

So far he's showing very few side effects, except for the horns and the unusually large number of flies that seem to follow him around. It doesn't seem to bother him though. He just swishes his tail and they fly off to Jay Cody's house.

Jay has been using horse liniment to cure his rheumatism. From what I hear the liniment not only has cured his aches and pains, but has also solved his receding hairline problem. He now combs his mane over it.

For centuries, the nomads of Asia used to bathe their womenfolk in mares' milk to keep them beautiful. The practice never caught on over here. Although occasionally we read of some movie star who soaked by the hour in cow's milk to hopefully halt the aging process. I once heard that Mae West had a milk bath every day. But in the hurly-burly world of today, very few Hollywood personalities can afford the time for a good soak in the tub and most starlets prefer to hang a cow from the ceiling and have a shower. (I know. That's a very old joke, but I was desperate.)

Personally, I have never felt the need to try any of this stuff. I read a few months ago about a winery in France that has a spa next door.

For a few thousand francs they'll soak you in a tub of wine and whack you with little sticks. That sounds kinky, and I might be interested in something like that. Not only do you feel better, you never have to buy socks again — as long as you like purple.

Well I have to go. Eileen just called. We have to take Pete out to Hewitt's farm. They've got a new bull. I wonder if we should give him a couple of drinks first.

Big business down the tubes.

The B. B. & B. Boutique faces bankruptcy

The Big, Bold & Beautiful Boutique is a store for plus-size women that opened in Toronto in 1987. It went on to publish a fashion catalogue and eventually start a web site that attracted customers from around the world. The company is struggling against the discount sales of the better-financed chains and department stores.

It's an old story really. So many businesses have gone under over the past few years for the very same reason.

I have an answer to their problems though, and that answer is so simple — hire a big name celebrity to hawk their products on national TV. I'm sure there are any number of stars, athletes, and politicians who would be willing to represent B. B. & B. Roseanne Barr comes to mind right off the bat.

I'll bet even Wayne Gretzky could be persuaded to dress up in drag to get him through the hard times. Now that he is out of work and barely hanging on until his CPP kicks in, I bet he might consider doing the odd commercial. In fact, I'm sure of it. When he called me yesterday to see if he could shovel my driveway, he sounded desperate.

I guess you've noticed that over the past few years a lot of movie stars and professional athletes have sold their souls to the advertising agencies just to make ends meet. June Allyson has been on prime time TV night after night discussing how her life has changed thanks to Depends.

And it did change, too. During the disastrous floods out west, it wasn't the sandbags and the Canadian army that saved Winnipeg. It was June standing bravely on the banks of the Red River with nothing but her courage, a snorkel, and a box of Depends.

Jane Powell, the great musical star, is another fine example. Although, she appears to have few problems with incontinence, Jane's dentures were in serious trouble. Then she discovered the miraculous cleansing properties of Polident. Today, you can go into her house any time and her teeth will be sitting there on the piano just a-sparkling. At night you can read by them.

The secret to success, of course, is to hire a big name personality who will best represent your product in the marketplace. It would be asinine to have Don Knotts telling the world how much sexier he looks now in an extra large peek-a-boo teddy than he did wearing his Barney Fife suit — although he probably does.

I think the ad agencies are missing the boat by not casting Canadian politicians as product spokespersons. After the incident on the plane last week, I was going to suggest that Sheila Copps would be an excellent shill for the World Wrestling Federation. But now it appears that the whole incident was blown out of proportion. I was hoping to see Tequila Sheila, our Deputy Prime Minister, tossing some handicapped person out of the ring and then screaming at him. (Wrestling fans really get turned on by that sort of thing. They're not all that bright and they vote Liberal.)

Mel Lastman would be the ideal man to advertise Brillo pads. Mel has to be 70 years old. You'd think his wife would tell him that Afro haircuts went out in the '60s.

Ernie Eaves could advertise Brylcreem. He gets his hair cut by the same guy who used to snip away on George Raft in the '40s. If he doesn't want to get involved in the ad business, he should try out for the next Elliot Ness movie. If he doesn't look like a gangster, no one does. Of course, working at Queens Park does that to you. I saw Garfield Dunlop on the street the other day. I'm afraid he might go to Ernie's barber and start looking like a hit man for the mob. Come to think of it, working for Mike, I guess he already is.

The lady who started Big, Bold and Beautiful, Jackqueline Hope, also owns three modelling agencies: Plus Figure Models, Petite Women Models, and the men's agency that is trying to hire me, Huge, Handsome Hunks. She got my name from Leon's. They were looking for someone full-figured to model sofa slipcovers and my name was on the top of their list.

An almost true story.

Last year's wieners, a jug of wine, and thou

Well, it's a big day on Bayview Parkway, Sharon decided we are cleaning out the fridge. I don't know if you do this at your house, but every year or so (depending on when the fridge door starts to bulge) we put on our work gloves and safety boots, alert the poison control centre, and dig right in.

Cleaning a fridge is an important event in most people's lives. Digging through the little Tupperware bowls and jars to find the back wall of the old Crosley is more than just housekeeping, it's a sentimental journey through the history of a family.

Sometimes we put on some soft music, crack a jug, and make an evening of it. It's so romantic recalling just when we wrapped that particular slab of salami that would be just the right size for tomorrow's lunch, or that lump of casserole that will make an excellent side dish some day. (Of course, it tasted terrible when Sharon first made it. I fed mine to the cat. To this day Duchess hasn't forgiven me, and hisses and scratches at me every chance she gets.) Old casseroles are like old love affairs; somehow they get better with age.

Over the years, the memory of that tuna casserole with the celery chunks and a spice that tasted remarkably like goat droppings becomes almost edible in the empty corridors of your mind. Those soggy noodles that you had to snap your head back to swallow, suddenly become ambrosia.

It's much the same as that love affair. It seems so sweet now that you almost forget that she called the police in 1979, and the artist's sketch of you that ran in the *Packet* under the heading "PERVERT LOOSE" didn't do you justice — especially your nose.

There's a square of something behind the pickles that may be cheese, although it seems a little porous. It might be a sponge that was left in there from the last cleaning, or it could be that urinal deodorant puck I put beside the leftover turnip. Someone ate the turnip (sure as hell, not me). Either that or the turnip mutated itself into a chunk of orange granite suitable for a doorstop or a primitive weapon.

There's a jar of red stuff with a blue-green mould growing on the top. We don't know what it is. It says "Aunt Mary, 1963" on the label. It might be jam, although Sharon seems to remember her aunt made chilli sauce a lot. It could be beets, though. I'd take it out to the Provincial Lab on the highway, but the last time they called the bomb squad, and we were detained for hours and frisked. I was humiliated. Sharon still goes back once or twice a week to thank the officer.

There's a jug of eggnog on the top shelf that we aren't sure is past the expiry date. Something dripped down from the freezer and covered up the date. (I think it was one of those orange freezee things we bought for the grandkids.) All we can make out is Hurls Dairy. I'd call them to see if it's still OK, but they went out of business twenty-five years ago.

There's a piece of wedding cake we got when two of our friends got married. The marriage lasted until she found out he had a girlfriend on the side and went at him with a machete. He was a good ball player. The Orillia Majors still use him as third base. She got two years. His girlfriend went back to her husband, who eventually ran off to be a circus geek. She was so depressed she joined the Liberal Party. We'd throw the cake out, but it's supposed to be lucky.

There's some leftover Christmas turkey wrapped in tin foil that I think I was saving to make soup. But we didn't have turkey this Christmas, so it might be chicken. We had chicken for Thanksgiving. No, Sharon says that was ham. It's hard to tell when she does the cooking. I don't know what in hell it is. I'll keep it for a few more weeks. If I can't remember, I'll throw it out or put it in a garage sale.

Now this is good. There's a bottle of red wine I hid in the vegetable drawer when some friends dropped by. I'll just crack this open and pour a couple of glasses.

"Now this is interesting, my dove. It's either baked beans or that stuff we mixed up to patch the driveway. Although, it could be those chicken livers we were marinating. Oh look, pepperoni sticks — or are they last year's wieners? This is such fun — more wine, my pet?"

I wanted to be an astrophysicist, but I couldn't spell it.

Chaos theory might explain our weather

I was reading an article the other day about Norm Murray. Norm is an astrophysicist from U of T who is receiving the coveted AAAS-Newcomb Cleveland prize for a paper he published about planetary orbits and the Chaos Theory.

We astrophysicists are always pleased when one of our own is honoured. (Actually, I'm not a real licensed astrophysicist. In fact, I thought they had something to do with a particular brand of yoghurt. But I know a lot about it.)

The Chaos Theory is relatively simple if you take the time to sit down over a few beers and think about it. It suggests that the smallest of changes in our physical world can expand infinitely and unpredictably in the larger universe. A fine example is the suggestion by noted meteorologist, Edward Lorenz, who just before they put him away said that the mere flapping of a butterfly's wings could set off a chain of effects that could change the weather. Anyone who has ever watched a butterfly and then been struck by lightning will certainly agree with that.

According to Norm's theory, planetary orbits are not as stable as everyone has believed for the last 300 years. They could take off without warning for no apparent reason. This could very well happen to us. One minute we could be sitting in front of the TV watching *Deep Space Nine*, and the next we are hurtling through it. That is a bit disturbing, especially if you have just spent a few hundred bucks on a side of beef.

According to his calculations, this isn't likely to happen for the next billion years. Nevertheless, I think we should be prepared. I'm going to go out on a limb here and predict that based on Norm's theory, next Wednesday morning about 11:30 or quarter to 12, or in the year 56,993,204, we are going to be catapulted by Jupiter at 5,000 miles an hour.

Fortunately, I have prepared a little list of precautions that we homeowners can take to ensure that this upcoming disaster causes little or no damage to our property.

1. Cover your outside shrubs and plants with a good quality mulch. I spoke to Bill Keller who is our local authority on gardening and homemade alcohol products. He suggests that a substantial amount of mulch should be distributed evenly over your flowerbed. Bill feels a layer 37 feet deep should be sufficient.

2. Make sure that your dog is protected from flying off into space. A fairly heavy chain will be necessary to keep Rover from blowing off the planet. The sturdiness of the chain will depend on the breed of dog, of course. A toy terrier will need something about the size of the anchor chain from the Titanic, while a bulldog or a Labrador retriever may require something a little sturdier. For my neighbour's dog that starts to bark every morning about seven o'clock, I would suggest a small piece of string or nothing at all.

3. Once you realize that you are hurtling through space (I'm sure that Bob McIntyre, the New VR weatherman, will let you know from his garden), you might want to close your windows and whatever you do, LOCK THE FRONT DOOR. You never know what kind of aliens might come pounding on your door with magazine offers or a real good deal on black topping your driveway.

4. Check your smoke alarms. If by any chance our new orbit happens to pass within 30 feet of the sun, a few moments warning might mean the difference between survival and shish kebob.

5. Keep a few cases of beer on hand just in case the Beer Store heads off in another direction. If you live in New York State this will not be a problem. A grocery or convenience store will be blowing by every few minutes.

6. Make sure you are wearing clean underwear. Your mother has worried all her life that someday you will be carried into a hospital and when they pull down your jeans, you will be wearing dirty underwear. Imagine how she would feel if you landed on a strange planet and your underdrawers were filthy — especially if you landed on Uranus.

7. Take a good book. It may take some time before you are rescued. I was going to suggest buying mine, but probably not. Take a big thick book with lots of dirty stuff in it. It might get pretty lonely out there.

Well, I guess that's about it. Oh, one other thing, Kirsten, our paperperson says, "Please pay for your newspaper in advance."

She doesn't want to have to be chasing you all over the universe every second Thursday.

How do Peter Mansbridge and Roger Abbott know if they are having a bad hair day?

Flyaway hair? Flyaway weight is my problem

I don't know if you read that Yale University has just completed a study on the psychology of bad hair days and its effect on a person's self-esteem.

I found that fascinating — not the results — the fact that some company would actually give researchers a grant to look into this stuff. (I wasn't quite so fascinated when I found out it was Proctor and Gamble, who by a remarkable coincidence were just launching a new line of shampoos and conditioners.)

According to the survey, if your hair is all ratty and you look like an unmade bed, you will feel less smart, less capable, more embarrassed, and less sociable. It didn't take too many brains to figure that out.

What I did find surprising though, is that it is men, not women, who feel dumb if their hair is messed up. Far be it for me to question the findings of Yale University, but I don't know too many men who spend hours in front of the bathroom mirror every morning with elixirs, gels, and conditioners. Nor do I know any who keep a medicine cabinet of exotic chemicals and sprays to combat split ends, frizzes, and flyaway hair.

Actually, I do have a male friend who does have a serious problem with flyaway hair. His flew away in 1974 and never came back. He still spends hours in front of a mirror, but not with sprays — with a can of Johnson's paste wax and a hand-held floor polisher.

My problem with the survey isn't so much the hair thing and the questions they asked, but *who* they asked — sixty men and sixty women from age 17 to 30. What do people of that age know about fly-away hair? And why should they even care? They should be at their peak of freshness — no wrinkles, no funny brown liver spots, and bet-ter still, no cellulite deposits, and love handles that have to be hidden under a one-size-fits-no-one beer shirt and baggy sweatpants.

When I was their age, I was a young Adonis. Bus tours came from the city every summer just to see me in my shorts. Robert Redford used to call me for grooming tips. Elizabeth Taylor would send me little notes to say that Nicky or Eddie or Mike or Richard (I forget the other nine) would be away on the weekend and was I doing anything. The Speedo Company began to drop off samples of their latest swimming briefs with lucrative financial offers for me to be their poster boy.

Charles Atlas let me kick sand in his face. The Pope wrote to sug-gest that if I must jog, that I not jog by the convents. One pass by me in my Speedo and he feared the young ladies would leave in droves.

But all good things must end. One day I reached 31. In spite of my Spartan diet and super-active lifestyle, even my powerful body began to show infinitesimal signs of wear and tear. My stomach, once a bronzed washboard of rippling muscle, began to take on the shape of the washing machine itself.

My manly chest lost its tone and the Maidenform Bra company began to send me samples. The Nemo Girdle people suggested that big money could be made modelling for their catalogue.

Suddenly I had jowls. I awoke one morning to find that sometime during the night I had grown an extra chin. (I offered to sell it to Joe Clark but he wasn't interested — a decision that eventually cost him an election.)

Andy, my barber began asking odd questions like "Would you like me to do something with those eyebrows or are you planning to comb them back over your forehead?" or making weird comments, "I see you are growing your own ear muffs." He's starting to talk about a tint.

I began to add even more pounds, although they were hardly noticeable. Although, now that I think about it, whenever I swam in Couchiching Park, I could hear giggles. Once I dove off the park dock and swamped the Island Princess tour boat.

My feet disappeared. (I know they are still there, I can smell them. I just can't see them.)

And now I read this stupid report that says people with bad hair days have low self-esteem. Preposterous! Flyaway hair is a mere inconvenience. I'll tell you what low self-esteem is.

It's the feeling you get when the Georgian Bay Tourism Association calls to ask for twenty-four hours notice before you go swimming at Wasaga Beach to give them time to evacuate Manitoulin Island.

*I never knew women wore long underwear. Actually, it sounds kind of
sexy. On the other hand what doesn't?*

Look for Jimmy's Secrets on a runway near you

Isn't it strange that no one ever admits to wearing long underwear?
Well, no one except us old geezers.

Of course, I don't wear them myself. I'm sure they would be a godsend when the icy north wind is whistling around my bottom-most parts,
but I have to protect my reputation as a trendsetter in men's fashion.

Imagine my amazement last week when I overheard two lady
friends discussing the welcome comfort of their winter woollies.
Under the provisions of the Privacy Act, I am not allowed to tell you
who those ladies were. On the other hand, there is the Freedom of
Information Act to contend with, and also the Public's Right to
Know. I'll think it over. If I feel that it is my duty to disclose this information, I will publish their names, addresses, and sizes at the end of
this column.

It has never been fashionable for members of the prettier sex to
wear long underwear — especially under pantyhose. Rarely do we see
Playboy centrefolds clad in bunny ears and long red woollies, or see
the models on Fashion TV strutting down the runway in skin tight

union suits. Nor is there a section in the *Victoria's Secret* catalogue devoted to heavy woollen drawers.

It's no oversight. The absence of suitable women's winter underwear is a plot by the garment industry to freeze the buns off Canadian women.

It is time that I introduced my own line of women's clothing to protect the female bottom from winter's icy blasts. Today, I am announcing plans for a whole new line of arctic skivvies: Jimmy's Secrets.

This very afternoon, I will write to Jane Stewart, the Minister of Human Resources, asking for government funding. That's assuming the poor dear hasn't gone bonkers listening to the ravings of Preston and his roving band of loonies and resigned. I'm sure that if I send her a nice letter and some flowers, Jane will give me a few bucks to start my new business.

I'll have to act fast. Some of my neighbours vote Alliance and will very likely put a contract out on me. The rest of the folks in the neighbourhood seem fairly normal.

Since I'm not likely to lure the top designers away from Ralph Lauren or the House of Dior, I'll design them myself until John Galliano or some other fruitcake decides to jump ship and join the firm.

For some reason, ladies in long underwear are just not sexy. Which is odd really since just one peek at the average man in a pair of long johns will drive women wild. I certainly can't think of anything that will fill a woman with desire faster than her 250-pound husband waddling down the hall scratching his belly through a set of flannel drawers. It isn't fair that the ladies can't scratch and do the same thing.

What Canada needs is a new wrinkle — a fashion break-through guaranteed to keep a woman's hindquarters from freezing yet still inflame a man's desire.

I have the answer, my friends: a scoop-necked trap door.

What happened to the traditional long johns with the four-cornered trap door that enchanted us for so many years is a mystery. They just disappeared off the shelves.

When was the last time you browsed through the winter wear section of your *Sears* catalogue and saw Brad Pitt or Leonardo DiCappuccino posed saucily with his flap half open? I'll bet it's been weeks. But that's no reason why it shouldn't be done.

I don't mean that I should enlist the bottoms of those two bozos — I need to hire a top female model to grace the pages of *Vogue* with the latest creations from Jimmy's Secrets — like the popular Rainy

River Rump Robe, or the soon-to-be unveiled Fesserton Frost-Free Fanny Flannel.

I'm sure that Naomi Campbell will take a few days off from beating up her employees to model for me. I might even hire Elizabeth Taylor to promote my larger-than-life lines.

A trap door with a sexy scoop neck is the perfect solution. It will keep Madame warm and toasty, yet still add a touch of mystery and intrigue to her relationship (or relationships if she, like Liz, is working her way through the alphabet).

It might even usher in a new era in women's fashion — rear cleavage. It has been done before. I'm sure the older perverts will remember Vicky Duggan and her plunging back line. And who can forget the dress Miss Ann Samantha Stevens wore to Bill Clinton's Presidential Ball? It was cut so low in the back you could see her initials.

(Apparently I won't be publishing the names of the ladies with the long underwear. Eileen said that if I did she would personally boot my trap door all over the City of Orillia.)

I don't know what I would do without the helpful hints column in the Saturday Star.

Plumbing the reader exchange for helpful hints

I'm sure that we all read the little helpful hints that occasionally show up in newspapers when copy comes up short or the reporter finally realizes that he or she isn't being paid by the word.

Often you'll find clever little suggestions — like filling up plastic bottles with water and freezing them to keep picnic hampers cool in the summer, or putting used Fleecy static sheets in your underwear drawer to keep your knickers fresh as a summer breeze.

However, the best ideas to make your life a little easier are found in the reader exchange columns. Here is the spot where so-called normal people mail in their suggestions on how to save money by using up stuff that most people chuck in the garbage or blue box. Some of these hints are quite clever, but most, I fear, border on asinine.

A while ago, I read some homemaker's brilliant idea of making toilet bowl cleaner by emptying the dregs of a Javex bottle and anything else they found under the sink into the can. The next week, a chemist frantically wrote that one whiff of her magic potion and Mrs. Clean's next work assignment could be scrubbing toilets for the heavenly host.

Sometimes these ideas not only seem too good to be true, but often they defy the laws of time and space. Today I read that a man has overcome the problem of jet lag by cutting insoles out of brown paper bags and stuffing them in his shoes. Granted he now looks like an idiot, but while the rest of the passengers are snoozing on a bench in Terminal 3, he is skipping out the front door all wired up as if he had just inhaled helium.

We all like to save a few bucks, but sometimes there seems to be a fine line between being thrifty, environmentally conscious, and just being cheap.

Today's hints:

1. I have saved hundreds of dollars over the years by making my own earrings. I staple the little empty packets of coffee sweeteners to kitchen garbage twist ties and thread them through my ear lobes. There are as many colours to match my outfit as there are brands: yellow, pink and even white — although admittedly I can't wear the white packages after Labour Day. I have even used aluminium beer can tabs for more formal occasions although we don't seem to get invited to formal affairs anymore — or anywhere else for that matter. I also saved money on ear piercing by borrowing the papergirl's punch. Granted I ended up in Emergency, but the holes are quite serviceable except for the whistle they make in a high wind.

2. Several years ago, I started making our own Christmas and birthday cards by cutting the back out from cereal and soapboxes. Then I crayon a heart-felt message. I think most people are quite flattered that I took the time to send them something so unique. Some are so overjoyed that they call and say, "You shouldn't have bothered." They even send us old clothes and the address of the nearest food bank.

3. When our twelve kids decided that it was time for my hubby to have a vasectomy, I did it at home with garden shears and a handful of ice cubes for freezing. Although by all the screaming, it must have been fairly painful, I no longer fear getting pregnant. Although that may have more to do with the fact that I haven't seen him for two years; he's on tour with the soprano section of the Vienna Boys' Choir.

4. Rather than pay good money to dress up the outside of our house, I wash old dog food cans and paint them in bright colours. (We don't have a dog, but dog food is loaded with nutrients and my kids will eat anything. If only we could keep them from chasing cars.) I use the

cans for all kinds of decorative knickknacks. Last week, I tied a half dozen together and hung them up on the porch. They make excellent wind chimes and in a gale they can be heard as far south as Barrie.

There are thousands more ideas that we can tap into. Write your newspaper editor today and demand that they carry a regular reader exchange column!

Thank you for your kind attention. Now I must get back to work. I make lamps out of old wine bottles. So far I've made over thirty. They don't work but I don't care. Doc McAllister has booked me into the Donwood Clinic to dry out anyway. Sharon can just sit here in the dark.

Believe it or not, this actually happened.

People taking charge of their own surgery

I like take-charge people — people who don't wait for doctors and surgeons to come up with new treatments and medications for their particular problem. They go ahead and cure themselves.

Heather Perry, a 29-year old British woman, drilled a hole in her own head and cured her myalgic encephalomyelitis all by herself. I'm sure that thousands of sufferers are overjoyed to learn that relief is just a 2 cm drill bit away. Not only that, they won't have to line up at a hospital to have it done, they can do it themselves in the comfort of their own kitchen or home workshop.

No more will they have to sit for hours in a waiting room reading that 1962 *National Geographic* article on the mating habits of the natives of New Guinea. (Actually, their habits sound quite interesting. We might try some of the kinkier ones. Although the wife is still not sure about the bone through the nose business.)

Home surgery is definitely the way to go — especially now that the loonies at Queens Park have decimated our health system. I know that the next time I have to have a by-pass, I'm not wasting my time waiting for TGH to find me a bed. I'll just lie down on the kitchen table and do it myself.

A year or so ago, I watched a triple by-pass operation on the Learning Channel. After I stopped throwing up, I realized that it really isn't all that difficult. Operating your own rib spreader may be a bit awkward, but I'm sure it's just like riding a bicycle; once you've cranked them open a few times, it will become second nature.

I'm certainly not suggesting that just any bozo can do his or her own surgery — only us brighter ones. Even then, the more complicated procedures might be a little tricky. Before you even attempt replacing your own aorta for instance, you might want to practise on a friend or relative — preferably one that you're not all that attached to.

To be honest, Heather's home surgery was not without a few problems. For one thing, she drilled a little deep and penetrated a membrane protecting her brain. Although, I suspect a person who drills into their own head could bore in almost a foot and a half before hitting any grey matter.

Nevertheless, she says she is generally feeling better and there is definitely more mental clarity. I wouldn't be a bit surprised. A great big hole in the side of a person's noggin would definitely relieve a lot of pressure. The fresh air alone would be good for her.

I don't know if Heather is married, but if her husband or boyfriend is wondering why she is so quiet some evening, instead of saying, "Something on your mind, my pet?" He can just pull out the plug and see for himself.

Cleanliness is very important in a home operation. If you are planning on doing a little plumbing on yourself, make sure that you wash your hands. You might also want to wipe the table off with a little Javex before you begin — especially if you have just cut up a chicken. (My wife says that's very important with chicken. We won't even sit down at Swiss Chalet without a bottle of bleach. If we are dining out in Toronto these days, we won't even pick up the menu unless we are in a full deep-sea diving suit.)

There is always the danger of infection whenever anyone has surgery. Be sure that your operating theatre is spotless and the breakfast dishes shoved well back out of the way.

You might as well know right now that you won't be getting much help from your healthcare professional. Most of them work on commission. It's bad enough that Mike Harris is trying to rip them off without you beating them for their finder's fees. However they might lend you one of their old anatomy books. If you are going to take out your own spleen, it might be a good idea to know what a spleen looks like. (I think it's that thing that looks like a yam, but I'd check before you yank it out.)

I guess that's about it. Oh, one other thing: home surgery might hurt a bit. Since you are going to be doing the work, you can't very well put yourself out. In the 1800s, a surgeon would give his patient a musket ball to bite on. Muskets are few and far between these days, so you might want to put a .303 shell between your teeth. However, it is important under Mr. Chrétien's gun legislation that your head is registered with the firearms department. One other thing, if you are going to try the .303 business, please don't point your head my way.

Another true story — well partly anyway.

Bathroom afflictions begging for a name

It wasn't my intent to turn this column into a weekly medical educational centre. Sometimes though, new information comes my way and I feel it is my duty as your healthcare advisor to pass along these titbits so that you too can stay on top of the latest medical technology — or in this case, terminology.

My wife was discussing a common medical condition with her doctor that inflicts much pain and embarrassment to the males in our society. That problem is "Toilet Bowl Neuropathy." In layman's terms, T.B.N. is the likelihood of a man's legs falling asleep whilst he is sitting on the john. Just why she was discussing this particular subject with her medical practitioner escapes me. Perhaps, Dr. Pallopson, whose name must be kept confidential, was trying to explain how he got the large bump on his head and why his pant legs were wet.

Evidently men who use the bathroom to catch up on the local news or delve through past issues of *Reader's Digest* are at serious risk of falling flat on their beak upon rising. (I believe it has something to do with cutting off the blood supply to a man's brain, which seems to be in the general area.)

What I find fascinating isn't that Total Bowl Neuropathy can happen, but that it happens often enough that some bozo had to come up with a name for it. There must be a whole raft of doctors with nothing to do but sit around dreaming up new diseases, while Mike Harris and Alan Rock argue over which one of them will be covered under the health system.

It occurred to me that there must be hundreds of medical conditions just begging for a name — if for no other reason than to enable sufferers to form a foundation and hold their own telethon starring Jerry Lewis or some other movie star who can't get work.

In the interest of those poor souls who wander the countryside with various unnamed aches, pains, and itches, I have invested several hours and a staggering number of what few brain cells I have left, putting a moniker on some of the more common conditions. Strangely enough, several of these ailments and conditions occur in the privacy of one's bathroom.

Toilet Bowl Narcolepsy: An all too common malady wherein the person availing themselves of the family's porcelain reading facilities drifts off around chapter three only to be awakened by someone pounding on the bathroom door. For some unexplained reason, Toilet Bowl Narcolepsy rarely strikes in a home with two or more bathrooms. There is a similar condition, *Bathroom Bends*, where the sleeper wakes up jammed face down between the wall and the toilet bowl. Usually a call to the CAA wrecker is required to rescue the jammee. Although occasionally two family members working in tandem with twin toilet plungers have been successful in freeing the patient from his or her porcelain prison.

I have a friend who scalded himself on his bidet. It really wasn't a medical problem per se, although it may have something to do with a lack of grey matter. The manufacturer told him he had been sitting on it backwards for seventeen years.

Patella Pulverate: A medical problem that occurs whenever an unfeeling architect or interior decorator has placed the toilet roll just out of reach of a stretching sitter, causing the poor soul to crack both his/her knees on a cold tile floor. If the victim is fortunate enough to have this injury occur while he or she is goofing off at work, they could be lucky enough to qualify for Worker's Compensation until their old age pension kicks in.

Buttocks Boil: A fairly common problem wherein a bather drops his or her bottom-most parts into a tub of scalding hot water. Why they failed to notice their feet were burning is a puzzlement. The resulting screams have been known to shatter windows as far away as Moose Jaw, Saskatchewan, and caused expectant mothers all the way to Lexington, Kentucky, to go into hard labour. (Actually I guess it would be hard "labor" across the border.) There is a similar condition called *Rump Roastisitis* which is when an unsuspecting bottom is lowered onto a piping hot sauna bench. A large spatula and a block of Crisco should always be kept handy for just such an occurrence.

Wilkinson Weed Whacker Syndrome: Perhaps the most baffling-bathroom affliction known to modern medicine. A man doesn't realize he even has it until he's staring into his bathroom mirror some morning wondering where all the blood is coming from. Then he hears his wife call through the door, "Oh my angel, I borrowed your razor to shave my legs."

This column needs no explanation.

Canadians forced to weather a bizarre spring

April 5, 2000

I've been sitting here for an hour staring out the window at a driving snowstorm. Actually, I've been sitting here hoping some school kids might come by and brush off the car. It's that or I'll have to send Sharon out with a broom.

I can't go outside myself. I put my snow boots away, and already I've piled something on top of them and can't find them. Last winter, I never found them at all and nearly caught pneumonia.

April is supposed to be the time of year when birdies sing and everything. (That has the makings of a good song. I wonder if Al Jolson is still alive.) It's the time for April showers to come our way. They bring the flowers that bloom in May. Instead of seeing crowds of daffodils, all I can see is a flock of robins dropping from the trees like dandruff on a black suit. The crocuses are peeping their little heads through the snowdrifts and I can tell they are angry.

The bright side is the leaves that I never got around to raking last November are once again hidden under the snow and my neighbours are no longer cluck-clucking about how lazy I am. It's not a question of laziness. I was hoping to see our MP, Paul Devillers, about having the backyard designated as a wilderness area or a wildlife sanctuary and get a government grant.

Paul has a lot of pull in Ottawa now that he's a big wheel in the Liberal caucus. He is one of the few people in the party allowed to see Aline Chrétien with her hair in curlers. I have met Paul a number of times and once I was allowed to kiss his ring.

This weather is too depressing. I think I'll just lie down a while. Maybe spring will come again.

April 6, 2000
Oh great! Now it's raining. Maybe I better call Bob McIntyre and get his long-range forecast. This change in the weather is disturbing me. Personally, I think it's an omen of bad times ahead. We've been stocking our basement with beer and essential foods like potato chips and onion dip. If the rain is still coming down this time tomorrow, I'll drive down to the lumberyard and see if they have pre-fabricated arks on sale.

I remember reading in the Bible that one time it rained for forty days and forty nights. We've got thirty-nine to go, then I'm bailing out of here. But I'm not going to take all those animals this time. Sharon has enough of a problem cleaning up after me and the cat without worrying about elephants and tigers.

April 7, 2000
Forecast for Saturday — SNOW! Oh joy! Oh rapture!

The scientists are saying this strange weather is being caused by the depleting ozone layer. Apparently, it's all my fault for using shaving cream from an aerosol can. I guess they are right. Every time I shave it rains. Last summer, the farmers out west were willing to pay my airfare to Regina and have me shave out in their fields. Two years ago I did just that, but I had a particularly heavy beard that day, plus I shaved my legs. An hour later Winnipeg was under 6 feet of water. They had to call in the army and now my picture is on the side of the Trans-Canada Highway at Kenora with a big red line through it.

I've been a little concerned that it was me who caused the ice storm that shut down the entire north-east last winter. I don't dare say anything in case I get stuck with the tab. The upside to the ice storm was Ottawa was shut down for a week and saved the country millions, but if I take credit for it, some yoyo will send me the bill for his portable generator.

155

Personally, I don't think it's the ozone layer that's causing the weather problems at all. I think we are being punished for electing Mike again. You would think we would have been bright enough to know we should never let a man run a province whose sole accomplishment in life was shooting one under par on a North Bay golf course.

Just in case you are wondering why I always smell of garlic.

Pesky varmints are driving Foster batty

I've got bats in my belfry. (Actually, I should say, "We've got bats in our belfry," but I'm still in trouble over insulting my wife's Broccoli-Noodle Surprise. So, I've decided not to mention her for a while.)

Sometime around four o'clock this morning, a family of bats started to move their furniture around our attic. I tried to shove the cat up there to evict them, but Duchess isn't any braver than I am and refused to go. My wife just mumbled something about a pair of wimps and went back to sleep.

To begin with, I am not afraid of bats — except the ones that fly in through an open window, then turn into a nutcase in a tuxedo with a serious overbite. Fortunately, there aren't many of that kind around. Of the hundreds of bats you see zipping around your backyard just as night is falling, no more than seventy or eighty are bloodthirsty members of the Transylvanian Royal Family.

Nevertheless, it's better to err on the side of caution and stay indoors — especially if you are inclined to be a few pounds overweight like myself and could be described as "succulent." If you really must go out to make a fast trip to the Beer Store, it wouldn't hurt to string a garden-full of garlic around your neck, and carry a wooden stake and a ball-peen hammer.

I'm sure that you have all seen horror movies with vampires flitting all over the place hickeying us common folk. If you've been paying attention at all, you will remember they almost always have foreign accents, and wear tuxedos and a cape. For your own safety, you might want to stay clear of anyone dressed in formal clothes after dark. It's for that very reason I have never gone to a Three Tenors concert. (That and the tickets are 150 bucks a crack.) Luciano Pavarotti looks like he hasn't missed too many meals, and if it's snack time at the opera, I don't want to be standing within an octave of him.

I've also never toured Casa Loma in Toronto. I'm sure it's safe enough, but castles are where these guys hang out. There's no sense taking chances.

My wife thinks I'm cowardly, but I never watch spooky movies. Ever since I saw *Abbott and Costello Meet Frankenstein* when I was a kid I've tried to stay clear of them. Not that us kids were chicken, but when I was 9 or 10, if we were going to a spook show, we always went to the Saturday afternoon matinee. That way we could walk home in the sunshine. Monsters are rarely seen in the daytime. Most of them are on steady nights.

I've got friends working the grave shift at the casino and they can get pretty ugly after a few days without sleep. If one of Tom Long's telemarketers phones them before noon, they get downright hostile. You can see the hair growing right on their faces while they are listening. Within seconds they go berserk, tear the phone off the wall, and threaten to vote Liberal or NDP.

But this isn't solving my bat problem. A friend told me to throw a bag of mothballs through the vent and run. All that will do is keep the moths away from their own tuxedos; what good is that? I'm not sure a naked vampire isn't scarier. Besides, the same guy told me to do that when a skunk moved in under our garden shed. Not only did the skunk like the smell of mothballs, he invited his friends in for a sniff.

This morning we packed up and went to the museum. The ROM has a bat cave down there where you can see thousands of the little suckers hanging from the ceiling waiting patiently for a blonde in a black negligee to fall asleep on the floor. (I've noticed in vampire movies that sleeping blondes are high on their list of delicacies.)

I don't know if you have ever been to the Royal Ontario Museum, but the place is fascinating. They have ancient soup bowls on display that are almost as old as McGarvey — although I found it strange that along the bottom in hieroglyphics it says "Microwaveable."

When we realized how many people were there just to see the bats, we decided to keep the family that live in our attic. We might as well make a few bucks off the little devils.

If you are ever in Orillia and want the thrill of a lifetime, why not drop by Foster's Bat Cave. Admission: $15.00. (Blondes in black negligees: FREE! Please see manager for details.)

Every now and then my mind shuts down. I wrote this piece on just such an occasion.

Chicken hatched whole new menu for man

This morning, I was rooting through the fridge trying to find something to nibble away at until lunchtime, which wouldn't be for another twenty minutes, when I spied a piece of leftover chicken just sitting there minding its own business.

While I was deciding if I could sneak it outside before Sharon saw me, it occurred to me that not too many days ago this tiny slice of chicken breast had been part of a living, clucking creature. One day, he/she/it (I don't think it matters really, chickens don't have much of a sex life) was sitting in the hen house checking the classifieds to see if the KFC had any openings, and by dinnertime, Henny Penny was the business end of a snack pack.

As I stood there entranced, I began to wonder — who was the first cave person to eat a chicken? What could possibly have been going through a Neanderthal's mind to make him decide to pick up his little feathered neighbour and pop it on the fire?

We would probably never have found out this priceless bit of historical data, had I not found this dialogue carved into a rock cut just north of Severn Bridge.

Oop: What's for supper?

Mrs. Oop: I was thinking about a potato — maybe a handful of goose berries for dessert.

Oop: Aah, not flippin' potatoes? That's all we've eaten for three straight weeks. We might as well move to Ireland. At least they have whisky.

Mrs. Oop: All right then, Mr. Chef Boy-Ar-Dee, why don't you get off your fat duff and find something? Why do I have to get supper all the time anyway?

Oop: Because I'm a man and cooking supper is what women do.

Mrs. Oop: What do men do?

Oop: Nothing, now that I think about it. Say, why don't we eat this here chicken?

Mrs. Oop: Elmer? You want to eat Elmer? What are you some kind of cannibal? Chickens aren't food; chickens are ... although Elmer might be a nice change. You want fries with that?

And so the Oops ate Elmer and he was quite tasty. Next they ate Spot, who was laundering himself in the living room in front of the parson at the time, and for a midnight snack, Bullwinkle, a fully-grown moose who wandered by on his way to the Lodge to catch the last call. From then on, everything that walked, swam, crawled, or flew was on man's menu. He ate anything. Eventually, his taste buds grew so out of whack that some of the lower orders began to nibble away on turnips and Brussels sprouts — although the turnip eaters never advanced past the "knuckles dragging on the floor" stage of human development.

For 10,000 years, man picked up anything that looked chewable, tossed it on the fire, and after it was suitably charred, scraped it off and ate it. Man ate blackened chicken, blackened fish, blackened buffalo, blackened cow, blackened squirrel, blackened aardvark, blackened ... well, you get the idea. Eventually, his missus began to cook and was soon experimenting with *Chatelaine* recipes. She began soaking things in marinades with exotic spices, even washing her hands for special occasions. Soon everything had a zesty flavour — even the aardvark cinders were tasty.

On June 6th, 1901, Gaston L'Esperance, a French restaurateur, accidentally dropped a chicken into a pot of water he was boiling to wash his feet and discovered a whole new way of cooking. Soon people came from miles around to dine on his boiled chicken, boiled fish, boiled buffalo, boiled cow, boiled squirrel, boiled aardvark, boiled ... well, you get the idea. People no longer burned at home. Families went out to fashionable eateries where they were served fine wines and salads made from plantain roots and other weeds. (A few people tried to boil at home but the technology was beyond them.)

Next came the oven, the steamer, and the electric sandwich toaster I gave my wife for Christmas in 1984 that she still crabs about. Finally the greatest invention next to the TV remote, the microwave oven, came on the scene. Now a housewife could ruin a dinner in a fraction of the time. Men began to cook once again, although they poured beer on everything.

The world was perfect — until May 24th, 1994, when some dough head invented the barbecue.

So we are back where it all started — blackened chicken, blackened fish, blackened buffalo, blackened cow, blackened squirrel, blackened aardvark, blackened ... well, you get the idea.

While I was thinking about all this, my wife came over to the fridge, took the chicken from my fingers and said, "Don't eat that chicken, Porky. I'm saving it for the cat."

I knew old Albert was losing it.

New light shed on Einstein's calculations

Well I hate to say, "I told you so," but I told you so. It appears that Einstein's calculation of the speed of light may be out by a few thousand kilometres per second.

In Grade 11, Bill Cunningham, our physics teacher, told us that light was flitting around the universe at 186,000 miles per second. (Back in the '50s we measured everything in miles per hour, bushels per hectare, or hangovers per jug, not the metric crap we have to work out with a calculator today.) I remember saying to my friend Len Deverell, at the time that 186,000 seemed a trifle slow to me. Len was the logical person to discuss this with of course, he often had his dad's '52 Pontiac and was used to high speeds. He was also a mathematical genius. Len was able to calculate the amount of gas in the tank so accurately that he always made it home. Of course his father ran dry backing out of the drive way in the morning, but that was his problem. When my sons did that to me twenty years later, it didn't seem quite so humorous.

But as I was saying about old Albert, I could never understand why the scientific world is so convinced that Einstein was a genius.

Look at his hair for heaven's sake! Surely a man with an I.Q. higher than his shoe size could have found a barber somewhere in Germany who could do something with that mop he had on his head. I've heard about flyaway hair, but his was ridiculous. It stuck so far out of his head it had to have it's own passport. I think he grabbed on to one of those electric spark balls at the Science Centre and forgot to let go. He couldn't tie a tie to save his soul either. I've seen pictures of him. Albert was no James Bond.

What is really scary is Albert's theories are the basis of our space programme. Well, not ours. Canadians are far too cheap to put money into rocketry and space stations. Our loose cash is all tied up in referendums and non-existent tax cuts. (If you actually believe Mike will actually give you 200 bucks back this year, you've been sniffing rocket fuel.)

Mark my words, one of these days someone will sit down with an abacus and prove that Albert's doodles were just B.S., and a sky full of satellites will rain down on us like rice at Céline Dion's weddings.

Apparently, researchers have produced light beams that are so fast they exit a gas-filled chamber even before they enter. That is almost the speed that a teenage boy exits from his girlfriend's house when he hears her father coming down the stairs.

The researchers say it is like seeing a man fall down on a patch of ice before it actually happened — a preview of the future. To be honest, seeing into the future is not all that remarkable. Married men have been witnessing that sort of things for years.

He no sooner walks through the front door when his wife says, "You're not going to leave your shoes in the doorway for everyone to trip over, are you?" just as he is taking off his shoes to leave in the doorway for everyone to trip over.

"You're not going to leave the toilet seat up again, are you?" is another.

Women have always been able to see into the future. I suspect that talent was in the rib that Adam donated to the Eve project.

A classic example was Anne Boleyn. Anne woke up one morning and to everyone's surprise called Don Harron from Norwich Union. An hour later, she was beheaded and Henry received 2 pounds 6. She didn't even have to have a medical.

But getting back to Einstein, Albert also postulated that gravitation was a determiner of curvature of space-time continuum. I haven't got a clue what that means, but the theory made a fortune for William

(Captain Kirk) Shatner who may have been the worst actor the world has ever known.

It worries me that eventually all scientific theories will be proven wrong. People believed the world was flat for centuries and almost everyone knows that it was round — except the Conservative Alliance and a few members of the city council. The earth revolves around the sun — not the other way round. E = MC squa—

Oh, oh! I have to run. My wife just fell over my shoes. I left them in the doorway.

I love modern art, don't you?

This piece of modern art is a real bummer

I'm sure you must have seen the picture in the Toronto papers of the photo artist in New York creating the first masterpiece of the 21st century — a solid block of barenaked people lying face down in the street.

What passes for art these days amazes me. I don't pretend to understand much of it. I often wonder though what the Great Masters would think, if say, Michelangelo or Rembrandt took a senior's bus tour and were dropped off at a Modern Art gallery. Van Gogh would enjoy it, of course. But what can you expect from someone who cut off his own ear? Why he did it is still a mystery. I suspect Vince found a hoop earring and didn't want it to go to waste.

As I stared at all these bare bottoms spread across a city street, I found myself trying to decide if it was meant to be art at all. Possibly, but it could be one more political statement about the shabby treatment our proctologists are receiving under the Harris government's penny-pinching health service policies.

It occurred to me that others might see this artistic masterpiece differently — like the poets of yesteryear.

What would have happened if William Wordsworth had stumbled on this display after an afternoon of drinking cheap sherry with Elizabeth Barrett Browning in his field of Golden Daffodils beside the lake beneath the trees?

THE BOTTOMS

I staggered, lost, along a street
Bestrewn with cups and shopping carts
When all at once I saw a crowd
A host of naked bottom parts.
From curb to curb, they gleamed like suns
A quite impressive rack of buns

Continuous as a Tom Long speech
A Stockwell rant, a Manning squeak
They stretched in never-ending line
Row on row and cheek to cheek
Ten thousand saw I at a glance
They mooned the sky, bereft of pants.

Policemen rushed with eyes squeezed shut
To circle round to block my sight
Lest I see another's butt
Of chocolate brown or snowy white
I gazed — and gazed, but little thought
What wealth to me the show had brought

For oft when on my couch I lie
Besieged with bills and cell phones ringing
They flash upon the inward eye
My heart doth leap. My soul starts singing
And then my heart with pleasure thumps
I see once more those naked rumps.

Ogden Nash would have said it much quicker:

While on my way to see my granny
I think I saw a naked fanny.

Or *Joyce Kilmer, he had a way with words:

I think that I shall never see
A bum as lovely as a tree
Except when lying in the street
Then I think they're really neat.

I asked Dave Dawson to run the "bottoms" picture instead of my headshot that appears in the *Packet* every week. But he said, "It's bad enough for our readers to have to look at one, without staring at a whole street full of them."

*When I wrote this column a while back, I thought Joyce Kilmer was a woman and thousands of people (well, Lois Deventer actually) wrote to tell me what a bozo I was. People should be more careful what they call their kids. Imagine Kilmer growing up with the name "Joyce." His mother probably made him wear dresses until he was married.

Surprise is the best weapon.

School buses, Snowbirds could finish off Yanks

Here it is the 4th of July already. Our patriotic neighbours to the south are busy celebrating their victory over King George, the Threeth, while we are up here wondering where in hell all this rain is coming from.

Americans are not bad neighbours really, but why didn't we finish them off in the War of 1812 when we had the chance? Our prime ministers' heads should be carved into Mount Rushmore today instead of old George, Tom, Abe, and Teddy — although Mulroney's chin alone would have taken up most of the hill.

Canada should have won that war. I was talking to a couple of old guards down at the B.S. table at the Legion who fought in the big scrap at Queenston Heights back in '12. They said we Brits were just a musket ball short of taking their whole country, but by the time our boys got through customs, the war was over and John Wayne was already starring in a movie about it. A few details of that war seem to be strangely missing from the American history books — like our troops burning Washington. On the other hand, the part where the Yanks burned York is missing from ours. (York was later named

"Toronto", which is an Ojibway word for "City whose mayor still wears an Afro haircut thirty-five years after it went out of style.")

It's not too late! We should attack now while they are shooting off their fireworks and each other. Defeating the Americans would be a snap — even if the word did get out we had declared war on them. By the time they stopped laughing, the Fesserton Fusiliers would be camped on Pennsylvania Avenue, and Jean and Aline would be eating poutine and grits in the White House.

We'll send both our submarines down the coasts underwater, one off the Atlantic Seaboard to wait for the Titanic, and the other to anchor off San Diego to hem in their fleet. Now that I think about it, I'm not sure our submarines go under water. We haven't spent much on our military over the last few years, and we haven't kept up with the technology. I think we still have the old kind of sub that just floats along under the surface and the sailors breathe through straws.

The Grey and Simcoe Foresters are ready. They've been practising since 1945, and are just itching to go into battle. Actually, they are just itching. They still wear those scratchy old khaki uniforms they wore during the war.

I doubt if our army has enough tanks and helicopters for an assault. Well, we have the helicopters, we just don't have anyone brave enough to fly them. Once they get above 10 feet, the whomp-whump-whump things have a bad habit of falling off. Chrétien is promising us new ones, but don't hold your breath. They are on his list, but right after abolishing the GST, so you and I will be long dead before they arrive.

Here's the plan! We'll load our troops into a fleet of school buses and cross at Niagara and Sarnia. They'll just mingle with the tourists and look sad. The American custom officials will think it was just one more busload coming back from losing their shirts at our casinos. The only drawback is we have to go this afternoon. If they haven't surrendered by midnight, we're in big trouble. The kids need the buses to go to day camp tomorrow. In that case, we'll have to wave the white flag and beg for mercy.

Of course, we could always hold off until January when our snowbirds are down in Florida. The Yanks will be surrounded. Can't you imagine how you'd feel if you saw a fleet of yellow school buses tearing down I-75 at 45 miles an hour and 2,000 motorized wheelchairs chugging north by Atlanta with their orange flags flapping and their white hair, or what's left of it, blowing in the wind? Hell, they'll throw down their arms and sign up for French lessons.

So we all agree; we go right now.

Unfortunately, I must stay behind. My wife says I have to cut the lawn this afternoon, and I have a prescheduled nap arranged for most of January. But if you are in the strike force, and if they ever let you out of Leavenworth, would you pick me up a bottle of Johnny Walker Black Label at the duty-free store?

There is nothing as inspirational as a set of bare buns on a tennis court.

Streaking makes a comeback — finally

On Monday, a man streaked Wimbledon. When I saw the cheeky little devil running madly down the tennis court to the cheers of the giggling crowd, with a grin on his face and a Bobby on his sunburned tail, all I could say was "Hooray! Streaking is back!"

I had forgotten the excitement of seeing some bozo humiliate himself in front of a stadium full of amazed and waving spectators. Can you imagine his dear mother sitting at home in her flat in Chelsea watching her little boy hobnobbing barenaked with the finest athletes in the world? She would be so proud.

"Come quick, Nigel. Cyril is on the telly."

Streaking is the one truly universal hobby. Any jerk can do it regardless of age or circumstance, from the very young careening down King Street in a stroller, to the octogenarian hobbling across Yankee Stadium in a four-wheeled walker.

A streaker can be wealthy like Conrad Black, or the very poor like one of his columnists, plump or thin, or perfect specimens of humanity like me.

Streaking is relatively cheap. All it costs is the price of admission. You don't have to fork over a king's ransom for expensive equipment — although a good pair of sneakers might be advisable.

Streaking is great for parents, too. There are no designer uniforms to buy and more important — NO TRENDY LOGOS. Your kids won't come home whining, "Johnny has a Tommy Hilfiger sticker on his bum. Can I get one? Please, Mommy, please!" All a kid has to do is pull down his pants and start running.

It's great for the summer holidays.

"Mommy, I'm bored."

"I know, dear. Why don't you take off your clothes and streak the IGA? While you are there, pick up a box of Kraft Dinner."

There are lots of advantages to streaking. You can play just about anywhere. Streakers rarely have to put down a deposit and reserve a ball diamond from the city or schedule ice time at the arena.

"Yes, Mr. Foster, we have a half-hour open between the Old Geezers' Pleasure Skate and the Little Tots' NHL Stars of Tomorrow hockey practise. That's 3:30 in the morning, January 3rd, 2006. That will be $500. Cash or certified cheque works for us."

I'm sure that streaking causes problems for others — especially for a husband who feels a little inadequate in the first place. And what is a cop supposed to do when he catches this guy — wrestle him to the ground? Although he wouldn't have to waste much time frisking him.

And if it was a naked woman darting hither and thither amongst the world-class athletes, could he tackle her without a matron? Catching a buck-naked sprinter is no easy task at the best of times. Ask any mother who has chased a soapy two-year old fresh from the bath down the street. There are so few places to grab a naked person, and all the accessible ones hurt.

As for me, I'm glad it's back. Streaking was one of those grand old traditions that was fast disappearing — like having a prime minister who speaks at least one of our official languages.

There has never been a professional sport that wouldn't have benefited from a naked person running down the field, the court, the ice, or standing on the card table to kill the boredom. Who among us hasn't wanted to sit in a hundred dollar seat in the SkyDome and say, "Hold this $5 hotdog and this paper cup of warm beer, my pet, whilst I drop my knickers and run barenaked to centre field and back."

Not too many, I'll bet.

My wife's friend, Bill Bolyea, streaked his cousin's wedding, which I'm sure impressed the mother of the bride. I mentioned that he was my wife's friend because my friends have more class. Although, it probably has more to do with the fact that mine all have love handles that are written up in the *Guinness Book of World Records*.

Streaking is not without its dangers, of course. Injuries abound. Years ago, all falling on one's bum on natural grass could lead to was a few grass stains and occasionally a snake bite, but skidding 20 yards on your rear on AstroTurf can cause blisters and abrasions that require hospitalization.

Had the chap at Wimbledon tried the same stunt here and got tangled up and injured in the net, he'd still be hanging there. He'd have no place to keep his Ontario Health Card.

Now if the Russians could just come up with a gas-fired engine for my underwear.

Fire up the Kunikovs and really take off

Weren't you just thrilled by the announcement that a Russian engineer, Roman Kunikov, has invented a pair of gas-powered boots that will allow you take 4 metre strides and reach speeds of 40 kph?

Think of what a boon these suckers will be for mankind — especially for folks in the senior citizens homes. No more will they have to rely on visiting relatives or school buses to drive them to the park or the local pub; they can just fire up the old Nike "Kunikovs" and take off.

"Good morning, I'm here to visit Mrs. Mertz."

"I'm afraid you're a bit late, she and forty-five other members of the Geritol Gallopers were last seen striding by Gravenhurst on their way to a rock concert in North Bay. If you have a Chevy Corvette you might catch them, but if they are drafting behind a transport, they're long gone."

My dad is 86 years old. I'm going to have him fitted. In fact, I've already got a call in to Lucien Bouchard to see if he's getting a pair. I can put the one he doesn't need on my dad's cane. I figure father should be able to make it up the basement stairs in about a second and a half — unless he misses the turn. Then we may have to add a couple of hours to peel him off the wall.

My mother doesn't need a pair. She goes 40 kph now.

The Russians say there have been no accidents so far. (Of course, they also said that Chernobyl was just an oversized microwave oven.) I'm sure that's true today when no one has them, but wait until Kunikov boots are in all the sporting goods stores and everybody and his brother has a pair. There'll be major smash-ups and rollovers all over the place. Can't you imagine Saturday morning at the A&P? Thirty housewives all racing for the express checkout so they can get home to make the old man's lunch. (Surely you don't expect him to get his own.)

I can see the front page now.

Thirty-cart pile-up in local supermarket

Police were called this morning to a dreadful accident in the pasta aisle of a local supermarket. From what investigators have managed to piece together, about thirty shoppers collided at 40 kph after the P.A. system announced an Air Miles special on Kraft Dinner. According to a sobbing witness, Mrs. Seymour Spotz was in the lead coming around the toilet paper aisle, but the wobbly wheel on her shopping cart disintegrated somewhere around 25 k's causing her to careen into the Classico Spaghetti Sauce display on the corner of Pasta and Pizza/Salsa/Tomato sauces aisle. Approximately twelve bottles of Spicy Red Pepper were last seen flying through the bakery department. Department spokeswoman, Marion Wilkie, said she feared for her buns. Damage has been estimated in the tens of thousands of dollars. Fortunately, injuries were minor with the exception of one man, a Mr. J. Foster who was bending over reading the label on a box of egg noodles when the collision occurred. Store management is still deciding whether he can keep the jar of sauce, once it has been removed. Trauma counsellors will be available to calm the husbands who missed their lunch. As usual, alcohol may have been involved.

As with all inventions involving gas engines, there will be environmental problems. The fumes and smoke from a supermarket of idling Kunikovs will have the potential to wipe out what's left of the ozone layer without any help from aerosol cans. The government will have to step in and put emission control regulations on your boots. Every five years you will have to line up at certified shoe stores and inspection garages and stand around in your bare feet. A licensed technician will stick his nose in your Kunikovs to see whether it's the fumes from your boots or your feet that are polluting the Earth's atmosphere. In my case, it will be my feet.

Of course, the big shoe companies will get in on the act and start to mass-produce them. Then the advertising campaigns will start. "Buy the new Michael Jordan Super Nikes* with overhead cams, ABS brakes and dual stainless steel pipes — guaranteed to hit 100 kph in 5.9 seconds or we will resole your boots and give you a free pedicure."

Jonathon Baillie move over, we're coming through!

*Removal of butterflies and other insects may not be covered under all dental plans.

Get out the old 78s and put on Perry Como.

All the fun falls out of raking leaves

I love the fall. It's my favourite time of year. The loveliest song is playing on the radio.

> *The autumn leaves drift by my window*
> *The autumn leaves of red and gold*

Stockwell Day won't approve of me working today; it's Sunday.
But I'm going to enjoy the beauty of the season and rake my leaves. I
can see them floating gently down, down, down to nestle softly on my
lawn. God is laying a rich carpet of crimsons and yellows upon the
earth to tell us that soon the snow will fall, and once again our world
will face winter's icy blasts. Our little furry friends, the squirrels, are
busy gathering nuts and my neighbour's tulip bulbs in preparation for
a long winter's nap. They chatter gaily to me as I get out my rake and
set a steaming cup of coffee on the front steps in readiness for an
hour or so of enjoying the wonders of this glorious season. I hear my
song again.

The autumn leaves drift by my window
The autumn leaves of red and gold

I think back to my childhood; those carefree days when we laughed and rolled in huge piles of golden leaves. Such wonderful days!

I have been out here about an hour now. It's great fun to rake the crackling leaves into a pile and — it's quite a large pile actually — maybe a few more than I thought.

I wave to Charlie Udell across the street. Charlie isn't quite into nature like I am. He has a giant 200 horsepower gas powered blower that can flatten a garage if it gets too close, and deafen someone as far away as Australia. He doesn't see me. He is busy driving big stacks of leaves and fallen debris on Theresa's lawn next door. Theresa is out. Too bad, really. I'm sure she would like the opportunity to express her thanks to him properly. I'll be sure to remind her when she gets home.

I don't know where all these damn leaves are coming from. I've been out here three hours now and my back is getting sore. I forgot the coffee and when I took a swig, it was ice cold. Plus a caterpillar or some other creepy thing decided to hibernate in it. I nearly threw up.

About an hour ago, a north wind came up. Not only am I raking and bagging my own leaves, thousands of the little suckers are drifting over from Lil's next door. I can see her in the window giggling. As fast as I rake, her tree pitches another thousand down. About an hour ago, I realized they were gaining on me.

Now I'm starting to get mad. I had a big pile built up by the road. Some lunatic in a truck came by and blew most of them back on the lawn. Maybe a whack on the side of the head with a rake would show Mr. Truck-driver-person that he should be more considerate of his neighbours. Come to think of it, he doesn't live around here. I think the jerk just drives around all day harassing us nature lovers.

I ran out of plastic bags and had to send Sharon to the store to get another stack. She bought a package of five. The flipping leaves that I dugged out of the window box would fill five bags. Perhaps I should have tempered my remarks about her lack of shopping brilliance. I heard the door slam. The windows rattled in every house on the street.

Where are all these leaves coming from? I've been out here seven hours now and I'm dry. I forgot to get beer this weekend. I asked you-know-who to slip over to the in and out store. Apparently, she isn't speaking to me. She threw the car keys into one of the leaf bags.

Another thing: while I was scooping up armfuls of leaves I hadn't noticed that a dog had been by for a visit. Not only am I cranky and tired, I smell bad.

It's almost dark. I've been out here fourteen hours now. I have just under a thousand bags of leaves piled up at the side of the road, but there's not one leaf on my lawn.

Omigod! The wind is shifting. Now Hughie's leaves are drifting my way. Go back! Go back!

There's that stupid song again.

The autumn leaves drift by my window

What kind of an idiot would write a song like that? Some jerk in an apartment building in downtown New York, I'll bet.

Did I tell you I hate this time of year?

I could not believe that the U.S., a country that brags it is democracy's flagship, could screw up an election so badly. It reminds me of a sovereignty vote in Quebec.

A simpleton's guide to exercising one's franchise

Once again it is time for all good citizens of Canada and the United States to troop to the polls and exercise our franchises. This year, however, the prime minister sneaked another election in on top of our regular municipal elections, so we will be exercising our franchises twice. The danger here, of course, is that we may all overdevelop our franchises and will walk funny.

Many people (well not that many really) have asked me to explain to the readers, who as a rule haven't a clue what is going on, the difference between municipal and federal elections, and in particular, just how our method of electing inept politicians compares to the American system, where the people they elect are far more inept.

The Americans have been holding elections much longer than we have. Their first election was held on July 4th, 1776, when the citizens, disguised as Indians, marched to the polling booths and threw the ballots, a number of tea bags, and several Englishmen into Boston Harbour. (This may not be quite factual. The day we took American history in Grade 9, I was lost in an erotic daydream about the girl sitting beside me that lasted until I was 60 and my wife found out.)

Our first federal election was held on July 1st, 1867, when Sir John A. MacDougall (something like that) asked for a standing vote in a Muddy York tavern. The last guy to fall down was declared the prime minister. His first governmental decision was to levy a tax on the rest of the citizens to cover the bar tab.

I have no idea when the first municipal election was held in either country, nor do I care. At one time in Orillia local elections were held once a year, then every two years. Now we are stuck with them for three years. I don't know whose idea that was, but he should be taken outside and dealt with.

There is a vast difference between the three voting procedures. In the U.S. federal elections, politicians put up signs, bore the heck out of us on TV, and generally screw up the TV schedules for weeks at a time. In Canada, the politicians put up signs, bore the heck out of us on TV, and generally screw up the TV schedules for weeks at a time. So you can see there is little similarity between the two systems.

In municipal elections, at least here in Orillia, the candidates bore the heck out of us. Fortunately, they are only allowed on Cable 10, which no one in their right mind watches. I say, thank God for small mercies.

The one factor common to all three electoral procedures is the "secret ballot." This is the basis of a modern democratic system and differs from the method used in some banana republics, where a person aspiring to a high office "secretly shoots" his opponent. This is, of course, very undemocratic, but it does have certain advantages. Not having to listen to five party leaders ramble on for hours about tax cuts and two-tiered brain surgery has to be high on the list.

The secret ballot gives us the right to vote for any idiot we choose and not be held accountable. It also helps to explain why Ontario elected both the Bob Rae NDP persons and Mike Harris and his Tories, and not a soul in the province will admit to voting for either one of them.

Canadians pride themselves in being on top of the candidates — perhaps I better reword that — Canadians pride themselves in studying the qualifications of the candidates and marking their ballots based on weeks of careful consideration of their past records and stated election platforms. That is why we have such fine persons representing us today.

I love to wander into the polling stations and listen to the conversations from screen to screen.

"Mary, who in hell is Norbert Cranston? Is he the guy we met at your sisters? Maybe I'll put my 'X' beside him."

"No, that was Norman something. Cranston is the one Harold says is a crook. I'm going to vote for Melvin Mugwump. I saw his picture in the *Free Press* once for doing something. I can't remember what, but let's vote for him."

It's a wonderful system and as free from political influence and common sense as you will find anywhere.

An explanation of astronomy for the simple-minded.

Meteor falling on Earth is so annoying

I'm sure that most of you have been keeping a close watch on the heavens, checking on the latest asteroid heading our way. At first, 2000 SG344, an object as big as an office building, was predicted to hit the Earth's atmosphere in 2030; a pretty scary thought if your roof needs re-shingling. However, it now appears that we are safe until September 16, 2071. Whether that is in the morning or after lunch is not clear. We better find out soon. Sharon shops on the weekend and there is no sense stocking up on cooked ham if we won't be around to enjoy it.

Giant meteors, or whatever, falling on Earth can be most annoying. A big sucker landed in Mexico 65,000,000 years ago and wiped out the dinosaur population. If we could pinpoint just exactly where the next one will land, we can make sure that our elected representatives are standing there waiting (heavily insured of course).

All joshing aside, what can we, the average citizen, do if we are out puttering in the garden and see a heavenly object the size of the SkyDome bearing down on us? Fortunately, I have had a fair amount of experience with falling objects. (I'm sure you remember my column a few years ago about a bird pooping on me in a Barrie parking lot. That was in 1996 and I haven't been back there since.) I have several suggestions. You might want to cut them out and stick them on your fridge.

WHAT TO DO IF A METEOR FALLS ON YOU

1. Pay your paper person. Just because you are squashed flat is no reason for some little kid to be out two week's papers. And leave a tip, it won't kill you — well maybe it will. Our papergirl, Kirsten, has already been around trying to talk all her customers into pre-paying the next seventy-one years. That comes to $23,444.20, if you take the Orillia *Packet and Times*. Although, the *Packet* is a little cheaper than most dailies, because we don't waste money on pruf-reeders.

2. Call the office of your local MP and ask if his or her party has a plan to reimburse you for any loss of income while you are lying under a 20,000-ton rock. If not, threaten to switch to the NDP; Alexa McDonut is always interested in social issues. If the Alliance is in power in 2071, we will probably have a two-tiered heath system. However, I wouldn't worry too much about any extra medical costs. When a meteor hits you, chances are both tiers will be stacked on top of you anyway.

3. Make a pass at that good-looking lady down the street. You know the one I mean. I've seen you peeking through the curtains when she walks by — and so has your wife. I heard her talking to her lawyer about it only this morning. Or if you are a woman, ask the stud on your block with the broad shoulders and jeans cut so low in the back that when he bends over he looks like a hairy Pamela Anderson in a scoop-neck blouse, to drop by for a cup of coffee or whatever. If you are a male and want to invite the same guy to drop by, go ahead, but I don't want to hear about it.

4. Call Don Harron at Norwich Union and ask him to put you down for $25,000. And while you are at it, check on their definition of an accident. Sometimes objects falling from the sky are considered Acts of God and are not covered. I'm still waiting for a cheque from my insurance company to have the bird poop scraped off my jacket. If it doesn't get here soon, I may have to get out a cold chisel and do it myself.

5. If you see a large object hurtling down on you at a 1,000 mph (or 1,609.4 kph if you must) it might be an excellent time to consider getting religion. Phone the church of your choice and ask them to

send you a list of their do's and don'ts, and whether they have any beliefs on an afterlife that you should consider. You might want to suggest they send the list by high priority mail. It may cost a few bucks extra, but what the hell?

6. Finally, and this is important, if the scientists have miscalculated and the asteroid is over your house right now, do us all a favour. Invite Stockwell Day and Jean Chrétien over for a quick drink.

A short course on editorial headline writing. Actually, I wrote it to make my editors Lisa Baillie and Dave Dawson feel important.

Americans don't give a hoot about election

Now that the American election is over and results discussed endlessly on every network from here to Hong Kong, I wonder if every news channel in the States will give the Canadian election equal time. I'm sure they will. Whether Jean or Stockpile, Alexa or Joe gets in is of the utmost importance to communities like Bugtussle, Tennessee, and Tombstone, Arizona. I can see the hillbillies now, gathered around the wireless fretting whether the Member for Kicking Horse Pass gets elected for his fifteenth time or not, and whether the poor man will have to retire on a pension worth more than the whole town of Bugtussle, including the chickens.

Our economies are so interdependent that the slightest burp on the New York Stock Exchange sends our financiers into a panic not seen in Canada since Queen Victoria forgot her birth control pills. In the same way, Americans study our newspapers by the hour to keep abreast of our every move. Americans care about Jean and Stockpile, almost as much as they care about whether Niles Crane will bed down with Daphne or not, or if Martha Stewart has found a new recipe for baked squash.

On their election night I agonised with the people of Florida that their vote was holding up the official announcement of the next president — almost as much as they sweated out whether Francis Smith would unseat Wayne Gardy in Ward One, or Melvin Mukluk would become the new Reeve of Cod Tongues, Newfoundland.

But most of all, I worried about the night editors of the hundreds of newspapers in Canada and the U.S who had to come up with headlines to hit the news stands on Election Tuesday.

Editors are the unsung heroes of the media. It is these poor souls who dream up the snappy lines that catch the eye of passers-by and convince them to cough up half a buck and buy the rag. Most people don't know that. They think headlines just appear out of nowhere and plop themselves on page 1.

Granted this latest election was a little off the wall, but editors have had to deal with delays and tragedies for centuries. Yet still they soldier on, night after night, coming up with fascinating one-liners. But do you care? Of course, you don't. No, you just sit in your easy chair checking the obits, without giving one thought to the editor who worked all night so that you could learn all the news you care to know from the headlines, before moving on to the comics to see what Charlie Brown and Lucy are doing in the tree fort.

Have you ever wondered why editors make such staggering amounts of money? Well, I have. I saw an editor's paycheque once and I staggered. Daily they practise their craft so that we can understand the day's events. Just think of the stories they have had to cover over the years and those unforgettable lines they came up with.

The Eden Daily Bugle, January 14, 0000
EVE DOES THE APPLE THING! ADAM HOUSE HUNTING!

Well, Eve did it again. This time she went too far and has been evicted from the Garden Estates Luxury Subdivision. In the meantime, her long-suffering husband is recovering nicely from rib surgery. Where one of them went is still a mystery. A reward is being offered.

Coventry Chronicle, November 21, 1042.
GODIVA BARES ALL!

Lady Godiva (Misty), wife of Leofric, Earl of Mercia, was picked up today by the Coventry Constabulary and charged with indecent exposure after she rode naked down Wimple St. to protest high taxes. She will appear before the magistrate as soon as her pneumonia clears up. Her horse, Ned, is charged with public mischief and littering.

Hastings Herald, June 16, 1066.
HARRY TAKES STICK IN THE EYE — DIES!

King Harold succumbed to injuries today after a Norman archer attempted cataract surgery on his eyeball. He leaves a wife, a cat, and a pair of safety glasses still in the original package.

London Times Gleaner, October 3, 1536.
QUEEN LOSES HEAD OVER ALLEGED AFFAIR!

Ann Boleyn (nee O'Shea) was executed today for apparently having a tryst with the Earl of Sandwich. Said grieving hubby, Henry, "Of course, I'll miss the little tramp. But what will I do for tonight?"

See what I mean? Headline writing is an art form.

I wrote this just before the 2000 election in support of Joe. Now that it's over, he can go back to sleep for another four years — well maybe three and a half or five.

It's High Noon starring Joe Clark

Whenever I see Joe Clark's picture I hear music. Oh don't panic, it's not a romantic thing. I hear music when I see Barbara Streisand's picture too — usually it's "I've got a lovely pair of coconuts!" — although admittedly, Babs and I have had a thing going since 1958.

But for Joe, I always hear the "Do not forsake me, oh my darling" song from the great western classic *High Noon*. I'm sure you've all seen the movie. Gary Cooper had to face five gunmen all by himself because his fair-weather friends suddenly remembered pre-scheduled dental appointments when the bad guys came to town. Even his wife, Grace Kelly, wanted him to vamoose and take up residence in Lafontaine or someplace a few hundred miles off the main stage line. In fairness to Grace, she was on his side, she just didn't want to see his name in the obits. They had been married only a short time and Gary was a prize catch. Already he had learned to sort the laundry and change his long underwear once a week. But even Grace left eventually. She ran off and married

Prince Rainier because he had lots of money and didn't wear his cowboy boots to bed.

Doesn't all that remind you of what his old pals are doing to Joe Clark?

Every day the papers bring news of yet another colleague jumping ship for the Alliance (and now the Liberals), leaving Joe to slap leather with Chrétien all by himself. It's *High Noon* all over again without the horses. Although, the whole thing has an air about it that suggests horses were involved — or at least the part the tail hangs on.

On the other hand, I'm sure Joe wasn't all that surprised. Politicians have very little loyalty and remarkably short memories. They'll swear allegiance to some poor sap today and the moment his back is turned they leave him for a guy with a chin.

Speaking of memories, I just shook my head when the Conservatives went berserk over Chrétien reneging on his promise to dump the GST; somehow forgetting that the most hated tax in Canadian history was their idea in the first place. When they got tossed out of power for it, the old guard and the media put the blame on Kim Campbell — as if Kimmy had anything to do with it. The Lord himself would have been turfed out on his ear for passing that one. If they had tried to levy a GST in the States, the Americans would have dressed up like Mohawks and dumped Brian and his tax in Boston Harbour. It's not just the Conservatives or the Conservative Alliance (I think that's what they call themselves this week). Both the Liberals and the NDP have been known to do a little blood letting and backstabbing over the years.

If political parties were families, they would have been labelled "dysfunctional" a long time ago, and all the MPs and MPPs sent for counselling or a psychiatric assessment. It would have to be on an out patient basis, of course, since the hospitals have no beds and would have to stack them on the lawn. Don't you find it fascinating that the Feds and Queens Park have trouble coming up with the bucks to fix the health system, but they can always find a few quid to run TV ads?

Maybe I'm getting old and crotchety, but I think I'm an average Canadian. I love this country, but I'm becoming very disillusioned and mistrustful of our industries and governments. I'm not a complete idiot; I don't believe the oil companies aren't fixing prices. On the other hand, I don't believe that a slew of it isn't tax. I don't believe that banks should be merging just to make a few extra billion at the expense of their employees. I don't give a damn if the TD and the

Royal are making record profits. When they are closing branches, laying off people, and hiring new employees for half the money and no benefits, they are doing a lousy job.

I remember when employees of big corporations were loyal to their companies. If they are loyal today, they're nuts. Employment Canada says there are lots of jobs around. I'm sure there is if you don't mind working twenty-four hours a week, for minimum wages, no benefits, and enjoy eating Kraft dinner seven nights a week.

Canada will pay dearly for this stuff some day!

Now I don't know much about Brazil, but haven't these people heard of Companions Wanted columns?

Mating habits of Brazilians fascinating

I read a fascinating article one morning on the mating habits of Brazilian women. Apparently, every Tuesday young ladies looking for a husband drop by Rio's St. Anthony's Church to ask the saint to send them a man. Although, that's not quite correct. The girls aren't all teenyboppers; some of the prospective brides are getting a little long in the tooth. I suspect that the odd one may even be 25 or 26, long past the age when a girl is still considering marriage. I find that once a young lady reaches her mid-twenties she has pretty well given up finding a bozo of her own and is usually satisfied with a granny nightgown, a cat, and a lifetime subscription to the Harlequin Book of the Month Club. When I was an eligible bachelor, I found that most women actually preferred reading romance novels to going out with me. I even tried showing up at their door with no shirt on and wearing a Fabio wig, but for some reason it didn't seem to turn the ladies on.

Now I am certainly not against lonely women asking for divine help in their search for a mate, things are tough out there, but I'm sure that this must put undo pressure on St. Anthony. I don't know what a saint does all day, but I suspect that going through the Rio de Janeiro phone-book looking for available men isn't his idea of a heavenly reward. To top it off, some of the ladies get downright ugly if the man he selects is not quite up to her expectations. Their revenge is quick and rather unpleasant. They stick their little statue of Anthony upside down in a bowl of rice or headfirst in a glass of water and lock him in a dark closet. (True stuff!)

Can't you hear the late Ben Hogan calling St. Tony to see if he wants to play in the All-Saints Invitational Golf Tournament and Mrs. Tony says, "Sorry, Ben, he can't come out today, he's upside down in a pail of water." I can imagine how long the newspapers would run those "Companions Wanted" ads in the classifieds if every time some girl got a loser, Conrad Black ended up with his head in a jug or a bowl of chicken fried rice.

Some of the Brazilian hopefuls are even fickle enough to get one man, discard him like an old shoe, and then have the nerve to ask Anthony to dig up another. Now that is just being plain greedy. Finding her a man was probably a tough job in the first place without having to scare up a replacement. What if she is one of those girls with purple spiked hair, a Harley-Davidson tattoo, and a ring through her tongue? How in the world is he going to get her another man? Tony was lucky enough to line her up with a blind man on the first go-round who wasn't all that picky, now he has to go looking for a man who's into the freaky scene.

These girls are not looking for a casual fling by the way. They are looking for the whole marriage thing, the wedding dress, church bells, and a man who has more than a pair of jeans with the bum out and a one-size-fits-no-one beer shirt in his closet. They are after another Pierce Brosnan, only one with a bit of class — an almost impossible task for St. Anthony now that I'm married.

Women ask too much of saints these days. They want him to find them some guy who washes occasionally; a man who can eat back ribs in a restaurant without having to change his shirt and pants before dessert; a man who doesn't have to watch every James Bond movie three times because it's the "Fifteen Days of Bond" festival on TBS once again. Well, forget it girls, that man doesn't exist. If he does, he must have some other bad habit, like trying on your underwear when you are uptown shopping. So don't go bugging St. Anthony to find you one.

One more thing — if you don't stop putting all this pressure on the saints, I'm going to write to Rome and ask them to take my name off the list. So there!

How would you feel if you found out you didn't exist?

This fellow really does have to get a life

The other day, a letter addressed to me arrived with my name scratched out and "no such person" written in ballpoint pen across the top. This is a little scary because the letter came from St. Paul's United Church. Churches have a direct line to the man upstairs. If St. P cross me off their membership roles, I could be in serious trouble. I can see myself standing in an endless line of heavenly hopefuls at the Pearly Gates waiting to be processed. St. Pete will be looking over his glasses and saying to Gabe, "Jim Foster? I don't have anyone by that name. Run him through that list of non-existent Quebecois on Tom Long's membership list. I'll bet you'll find him in there."

My chances of getting in will be slim enough without having the post office conspiring against me.

I should have realized I didn't exist a long time ago. All the signs were there. I never get any mail. If anything comes to our house, it's always addressed to Sharon or "occupant."

I get letters from the city, but they are addressed to "To Whom It May Concern." (They keep asking me not to put my *Playboy* magazines in the blue box. The driver has been pulling around the corner and looking at the pictures until quitting time. Ordinarily, that wouldn't be so bad, but we are his first call. You can't see the rest of the houses on our block for piles of old newspapers and empty whisky bottles.)

Even Publishers Clearing House has never heard of me, and everyone in the world is on their mailing list. Ed McMahon sends everything to our house addressed to "Dear Sir or Madam." His last letter said, "Whoever you are, you don't exist, and haven't a snowball's chance in hell of winning a million dollars."

Once I got a refund cheque from Revenue Canada. When I tried to deposit it at the TD the lady said, "The cheque is OK, but you aren't. Let me see some ID." I didn't have any. The postal person had gone into my wallet and written "no such person" on my driver's license — although I noticed the licence bureau was quick to take my 50 bucks on my birthday. The clerk made me comb my hair and stand up against a wall while she took my picture. I can hardly wait for my new license to come to see if my photo turned out. (I was going to say, "come in the mail" but, of course, it never will because it was the post office that decided to do away with me in the first place.) If my license comes with just a blank where my picture is supposed to be, I'll know they are right and I'm a goner.

I've been afraid to look in a mirror since all this happened. I don't know if I have a reflection or not. If you have no reflection it means you are a vampire or don't exist anymore — like Joe Clark and Preston Manning. Lately, I've been hiring neighbours to stand in our bathroom and look in the mirror while I shave.

Even the banks are in on it. Yesterday, I swiped my debit card through the thingy at the liquor store. Their whole computer system ground to a halt. The screen flashed "You've got to be kidding," and I found myself standing out on the parking lot with an empty bag in my hand.

Lately, I've been getting phone calls from telemarketers at dinnertime asking to speak to a Meester Jeemes Foster. When I say, "Speaking," they sound surprised and hang up on me. Don Harron called from Norwich Union to say that everyone in Canada qualifies to buy life insurance except me.

At the Scottish Festival a few weeks ago, I was talking to 10,000 people in the park and I realized no one was listening. Although, I'm used to that, I'm married.

This morning I was sitting in a parking lot. The police came and towed my car away. They thought it had been abandoned.

While I was bemoaning all my troubles to my wife, she said, "I don't know whether you exist or not either. But in the meantime, whoever you are, make yourself useful and take out the garbage."

I try to help at Christmas each year with helpful suggestions for the belea-guered shopper without a dime in his pocket or a brain in his head.

Cheap but tasteful gift will enchant ladies

This column is for the man who has suddenly realized it's December and that some time in the next month or so he may have to buy his beloved a Christmas present.

I have no problem with a woman reading this. For one thing, it will be reassuring for her to know that at least one man understands the way women think. The down side is she will have to act surprised when she sees the very gift she treasures most under her tree. In fact, you ladies may want to cut this out, and paste it to the fridge door or a beer case to make sure the bozo reads it.

Most of us old geezers with years of experience charming women long ago mastered the art of buying just the right gift to enchant a fair lady. A cheap, but tasteful card with a note tucked inside saying, "Here's 5 bucks; buy some new underwear. The bum is out of the pair you are wearing," is always appreciated.

(You older chaps can now go back napping through Matlock.)

Today, I've decided to help the young man just starting down the road to romance, who at this very moment is trying to decide what he can buy to show the girl of his dreams that he really cares, and that he is not just some inconsiderate bonehead like her last boyfriend, who gave her a peek-a-boo bra, which she opened it in front of her family, and her mom started to cry, and her dad got mad and threw the boy out the front door, and sent her to her room, and she set fire to the house and the police came and the New VR ... well, I don't need to say any more. We've all had that happen.

Women, particularly young women anxious to leave the family home and have her own bathroom, are surprisingly not all that interested in getting cooking utensils from their beloved. I found that out the hard way. I bought my wife a sandwich toaster when we were still dating. That was not a particularly good move. I know I have mentioned this on a number of occasions, but I guess a near death experience like that never really leaves your mind. Even now, twelve years later, I still hear her mumbling in her sleep, "Imagine, a G-D— sandwich toaster!"

No, my friends, stay away from cookery. For some reason the modern woman wants a more personal present, something meaningful that she can hardly wait to show her friends. I have just the gift.

"Guess what that loveable scamp, Algernon, bought me? ... a nose hair trimmer."

Think of the reaction you'll get as the two of you cuddle amongst the pressure cookers and fondue pots her poor mother got, and she says, "Oh Algernon, what a thoughtful gift. What ever made you think of it?"

And as you brush away her tears of joy you can say, "I don't know. Maybe it's the way your nose hairs suck up the butter when you are eating corn, or everyone laughs when you sneeze and your nose whistles."

Put that at the top of your list, lads: a nose hair trimmer. It's a crackerjack of a gift and — this is really important — it's cheap.

One thing you will learn over the years of dating and marriage is that women always say, "Now don't run out and spend a lot of money on me." She will be so pleased that you didn't try to buy her love and affection with something as crass as jewellery or designer clothes. A $12 nose hair trimmer will show her that not only do you love her, but also you listen.

Quite often men think intimate lingerie turns women on, and if you pour enough booze into them (the women not the lingerie) they might even model it for you. Au contraire, mon ami, au contraire. Give a woman thong underwear and she will think you are a perverted little weasel who only wants her for her body. Which in your case is probably true. Whatever you do, don't blow a month's pay in the *Victoria's Secret* catalogue. If you must buy her underwear, buy her something sturdy that will last forever.

When she opens her little package on Christmas morn and holds up a huge pair of flannel bloomers, she will certainly be at a loss for words.

Maybe add a little note: "Dear Rosebud, I realise these are a few sizes too large. But the way you've been packing on the beef lately, I'm sure you'll be squeezing into these babies in no time at all."

Let me know how you make out!

Of course, we can't forget the ladies who are looking for just the right gift for the fat guy lying on the couch.

Christmas gift ideas for your little Dickens

Dear Mr. Foster,

Last week you were kind enough to write a column of helpful hints for the men in our community looking to buy practical, yet exciting gifts for the women in their lives. I realize you must be under a great deal of pressure with your own Christmas shopping, but would you be ever so sweet and jot down a few gift suggestions that a befuddled woman could buy for the man of her dreams? While you are at it, please suggest something I can buy for my husband.

Lulubelle McConnell.

Dear Lulubelle,

How inconsiderate it was of me not to remember that occasionally women shop for Christmas gifts. Although, it is rare that a woman does much during the Christmas season except drink eggnog and pick away at the turkey giblets her husband has so kindly prepared for her. At our house, I have started to let Sharon get involved in the Christmas celebrations, and have entrusted her with the minor chores like shopping for the grandchildren, the family, and the few friends we have who didn't vote Alliance.

I look after the more complicated duties around the Christmas season — like buying beer. She enjoys it immensely and welcomes the chance to wade through snowdrifts and surly crowds of last-minute shoppers. Often when she gets home and I am still lying on the couch, I can hear her mumbling away about what a fine time she had and occasionally mentioning other things involving the Lord's name.

Yes, I will be glad to suggest a few things in hopes that at least one male reader gets something he likes instead of the usual fish tie and ankle socks with no elastic. By the time he has walked to the beer fridge, his cheap socks are bunched around his toes like drunks at a free bar and he has a bunion as big as an auk egg.

I think I can be reasonably sure there isn't a man alive who wouldn't be overjoyed to tear open a brightly wrapped package and find a pair of red thong underwear. Ever since the first volley was fired in the sexual revolution, men have been dying to wear sexy underwear that were previously only worn by fashion models like Naomi Campbell and Roseanne Barr — or those big burly guys in the leather suits at the head of a Gay Pride Parade. Your beloved's membership at the YMCA will be cancelled toute de suite, of course, but he will finally have that fifteen minutes of fame we all have been waiting for — although in his case it may last seventy years.

Think baggy sweat pants! Now there is a gift that every man will appreciate. Sweat pants (the kind that he can pull right up over his pot belly) are just about the most practical gifts one can give to a man. He can wear them — and will — in the back yard, to the curling club, to the A&P. He can even wear them when he goes to the mall to sit on a bench while you shop and pretend you don't know him. With any luck at all, you can sneak home without him. Sweat pants are an ideal Christmas gift for the man in your life because they are sort of one-size-fits-all and once on, he will never take them off. They are even washable if you can ever get him down on the floor at the laundromat long enough to whip them off and throw them in the old Bendix.

Is your stud-muffin a handyman? Perhaps a power tool of some sort would be the ideal gift to keep him in the basement whenever you have the girls over for tea or bridge. If he is not all that adept with power drills and saws, it might be advisable to do an inventory on his fingers and toes on Christmas morning. Jot that number down on a sheet of paper and drop it in the mail to the company carrying your Home Owner's Insurance.

Let's sum up, shall we? Thong underwear, baggy pants, and power tools. Yep, that pretty well does it. Any of these three excellent gifts will do.

But if you really want to make him happy on Christmas morning, slip into your sexiest negligee. Once your beloved is down in the basement, with his new thong drawers riding up his bum under his baggy pants and sawing away at a piece of lumber as big as the main support beam in the SkyDome, tap him gently on the shoulder and say, "Merry Christmas, you little Dickens."

Call 911 immediately!

It just wouldn't be Christmas if I didn't take another run at poor old Ebby.

God save everyone from Ebeneezer Scrooge

Scrooge was better than his word. He did it all, and infinitely more; and to Tiny Tim who did not die, he was a second father. He became as good a friend, as good a master, as good a man, as the good old city knew, or any other good old city, town, borough, in the good old world.
Charles Dickens 1812-1870

Sure Scrooge had a fine time. But what was it like for everyone else?

Christmas at the Cratchet's, 1853
(Ten years after Ebenezer's amazing transformation.)

Bob: A toast! To Mr. Scrooge, the founder of the feast.

Mrs. Cratchet: Bob, not Scrooge. If I hear that man's name one more time, I'll scream.

Bob: I know, my dear. But it's Christmas. I guess it hasn't turned out all that well, has it?

Tiny Tim: Tell me about it. I'm 18 years old and everyone thinks old Ebby and I are Siamese twins. Every time I turn around, the old geezer is standing there saying, "Well Timmy, my lad, what are we going to do now?" I can't stand it anymore. Last night, I had a date with old Fezziwig's granddaughter. When I leaned over to kiss her, I laid a smooch on old Ebby's ear. He stuck his head in between us. "Just to say, hello," he said. The man is driving me bonkers.

Bob: I know, I know. Ever since he saw those damn ghosts our life has been a living hell. For ten years the old coot paid me 15 shillings a week and we were happy as clams. Now I'm vice president of marketing. I make 1,000 pounds a year with stock options. Every financial planner in London is on my tail with another investment scheme and the income tax department audits me twice a week.

Mrs. Cratchet: What about me? We lived in a one-room shack and it was wonderful. Now we live in a sixteen-room mansion. We've got butlers and maids running all over the damn place. I used to love to make my own Christmas pudding. Now the cook won't let me in the kitchen. You're never home, Bob. When was the last time we made love — 1848? If it wasn't for Mr. Bumble, the gardener, I don't know what I'd do.

Bob: I'm sorry, pet, I know you are lonely, but I have to work at the office until midnight every night. I'm just too tired. Thank heavens Penelope Pickwick stays after hours just to help out or I'd never get home at all. She's such a wonderful secretary. She's even agreed to go to Spain with me for a week to handle my odds and ends in the Madrid merger.

Tiny Tim: Is she the one with the big ...

Bob: Shouldn't you be doing your homework, young man? By the way, where's our Martha?

Mrs. Cratchet: Who knows where she is? After Scrooge gave her that apartment we never see her. She's been married three times in the past six years. You know what we used to call girls like that when I was younger, Bob?

Tiny Tim: A hooker?

Mrs. Cratchet: That's enough out of you, Master Timothy Cratchet. Go clean up your room. Last night, I tripped over your crutch and nearly broke my leg.

Bob: If you fell, my love, you probably would have. You're getting to be quite a big bruiser, my angel.

Mrs. Cratchet: You would be too if all you had to do was sit around eating chocolates and drinking sherry all day. The only exercise I get is ringing the butler's bells. I suppose the old goat is coming over for dinner again tonight.

Bob: Not tonight. He's dining at his nephew Fred's. Fred can't stand him either. They never saw hide nor hair of him for ten years, now he's a permanent fixture. Fred's wife, Myrtle, said the decorator thought he was part of the furniture and sat a fern on him. He's carried this Christmas reformation thing way too far. We've had a scotch pine in the office since last January and the whole place is jammed with live turkeys. He gives them to the poor people. It's not safe to walk in there without rubber boots. It's even worse at Fred and Myrtle's. Myrt says she was having a shower and when she opened her eyes, the old weasel was standing in front of her holding a sprig of mistletoe over her head.

Tiny Tim: I don't blame him. I've seen Myrt. She's got big ...

Mrs. Cratchet: That's quite enough out of you, young man.

Knock, Knock

Mrs. Cratchet: Oh, please God, not him. Peek out the window, Bob.

Bob: My dear, it's Ebenezer. He must be here for dinner. Well, we might as well finish the toast. To Mr. Scrooge.

Tiny Tim: God save us! God save us everyone!